# Game Theory for Business

# Game Theory for Business

## A Primer in Strategic Gaming

by Paul Papayoanou

Probabilistic Publishing

Editors: Dave and Debbie Charlesworth
Cover Design: Heather Reitze

Initial printing: December, 2010
Second printing: February, 2011


Probabilistic Publishing

Florida:
352-338-1789

Texas:
1702 Hodge Lake Ln
Sugar Land, TX 77478
281-277-4006
www.decisions-books.com
e-mail: dave@decisions-books.com

Written, designed, and printed in the United States of America.

Library of Congress Control Number: 2010942593

ISBN: 0-9647938-7-3
ISBN 13: 978-0-9647938-7-3

*For Claudia, Alex, and Nash*

# Game Theory for Business and Strategic Gaming

"Strategic Gaming enabled me to see the chess pieces from right on top rather than from sitting behind my pieces. It helped me shape the competitive landscape at a pivotal time for my company and changed the whole way I think about my business."—*Gene J. Gebolys, President and CEO, World Energy*

"Understanding how the actions of other players (e.g., partners, competitors, governments, customers) can impact your own decisions is increasingly critical to good decision-making and project success. Although there are many excellent books on game theory, I haven't found one that effectively ties the theory to real world business decisions. *Game Theory for Business* does just that; it provides a practical approach to incorporate game theory into sound business decision-making."—*Frank Koch, Decision Analysis Practice Leader, Chevron*

"Strategic Gaming stands out as the first truly rigorous yet practical application of game theory. It has been refined by Dr. Papayoanou over the years through client projects that often result in startling insights unavailable with traditional approaches. Strategic Gaming fills a gaping hole in strategy development for real-world competitive-cooperative dilemmas. Next generation strategic thinking is now here."—*Brian Hagen, Ph.D., Managing Director, Decision Empowerment Institute*

"Game theory has, at long last, lived up to its academic promise in the business world. Unlike qualitative or black-box approaches to game theory, Strategic Gaming provides a straightforward, transparent, and rigorous way of applying game theory to generate valuable insights to many critical business issues. A must read from the leading thinker and practitioner of applied game theory."—*Steve Galatis, Associate Director, Portfolio and Asset Strategy, Bristol-Myers Squibb*

"Dr. Papayoanou's Strategic Gaming approach truly brings clarity to the decision maker. Its compatibility with decision analysis makes it a logical and natural enhancement to an executive's analytical toolbox. The transparency of the dialog and sequential progression throughout the process facilitates alignment of all participants."—*Larry Neal, Jr., Manager, Decision Analysis Consulting, Chevron Corporation*

# Preface

I was a professor for more years than I care to confess. But then I wanted to do something more practical and rewarding for myself and for others. I decided to leave academia and venture into the business world. I thought I could use my knowledge and skill with game theory, a tool I used as an academic, to help companies make better strategic decisions. After all, in academia game theory is widely considered to be the leading tool for gaining insight into competitive and cooperative dilemmas, which most companies face regularly. So I crafted a simple and practical approach for using game theory, now called Strategic Gaming, and started a consulting practice.

In developing my niche consulting practice, I talked with many consultants and business people and had the good fortune to work on some very interesting projects. I was heartened to discover that my offering could provide great value to clients—indeed, greater value than I ever expected.

Yet I was also amazed to learn that many companies were all too willing to avoid thinking seriously about action-reaction dynamics, leaving significant value on the table. As a former academic, it was hard to believe that strategic decisions and deals worth tens or hundreds of millions of dollars, even billions, are often left to guesswork, instinct, and rules of thumb rather than careful strategic analysis.

This reality cut two ways for me. On the one hand, it provided opportunity. If every, or even most, companies were rational profit-maximizers (as economic texts assume they are), and if they had the appropriate tools at their disposal, there would be little need for my services. Companies would think through their strategic alternatives and choose optimally. Indeed, this was the type of underlying assumption behind the academic work I produced in my previous career. In the business world though, I found such an assumption to be far from the truth, so there were clear business opportunities.

With Strategic Gaming, I could help my clients find and exploit strategic advantages to realize substantial added value.

On the other hand, this reality meant that selling my services could prove to be very difficult. All too often, executives, managers, and negotiators were more than willing to act in a suboptimal manner. Major negotiations and strategic decisions would be left to water cooler conversations, intuition, and guesswork. Many told me that little more could be done given the situation's complexities, uncertainties, and/or time constraints. In other cases, executives were content to stick with the "same old" tools and approaches; it did not matter that these methods could not adequately surface and analyze action-reaction dynamics.

Yet some wanted to try my game-theoretic approach and hired me. These clients viewed Strategic Gaming as a vast improvement over their standard approaches to strategy and negotiations. Time and again these clients said that Strategic Gaming gave them structure, clarity, and valuable strategic insights they would not otherwise have realized. Clients learned to think and act more strategically and to capture great value because Strategic Gaming helped them to shape and play the game of business more effectively. The benefits even extended beyond particular engagements–the approach had far-reaching and long-term implications for the way many clients approached their businesses. As one client commented, "This changed the whole way I think about my business."

This book demonstrates how Strategic Gaming has, can, and should be applied to help executives, managers, and negotiators develop robust, high value strategies and tactics. While there are a few books that discuss how game theory should be used to make business decisions, none elucidate a practical process for doing so. This primer details how Strategic Gaming can be applied in the business world to help large and small companies in a wide range of industries. With this primer, savvy strategists and negotiators will see that there is a practical methodology for shaping and playing the game of business effectively.

# Acknowledgments

I might never have gotten Strategic Gaming off the ground if not for my first client, Gene Gebolys of World Energy Alternatives. Gene is one of the most savvy executives and negotiators I have ever met, and he offered to be my guinea pig when I started out and when his startup was at a crucial crossroads. Our work together and Gene's business acumen helped World Energy Alternatives shape the U.S. biodiesel game, enabling the company to grow nearly twenty times in two years, becoming the clear leader in its market. Gene has since extolled the virtues of Strategic Gaming in public, saying how it helped him to see the competitive landscape clearly and quickly, and to act proactively so that his company could be a step ahead of others in his industry. Working with Gene made me realize that Strategic Gaming had great value even for the best in business; in fact, the best in business benefit the most.

My appreciation extends to many other clients as well, though I will not divulge their names to protect confidentiality concerns. In applying Strategic Gaming to their fascinating and challenging business issues, and talking with them about their companies' needs, I learned a great deal about where and how to best use the approach.

I am extremely grateful to various business associates over the years, only a few of whom I will note here. I want to thank Steve Galatis in particular for his support, friendship, insight and brilliant work on Strategic Gaming applications over the years. I would also like to thank Jay Goldman and Jan Paul van Driel for their unflagging enthusiasm and support in the early years of Strategic Gaming; Strategic Gaming would not have prospered without them. I am grateful to Brian Hagen as well for encouraging me to write this book, his keen insights, and his work with me.

Though I left academia many years ago, I feel obliged to thank two of my mentors in graduate school at UCLA, George Tsebelis and Arthur Stein. George patiently taught me most of what I know about game theory, and helped me think about its applicability to real world situations. Art strongly encouraged my use of game theory and helped me understand where, when, and how game theory could provide valuable insights. The lessons they taught me years ago guide me daily.

I thank Heather Reitze for the great graphics work she has done for my firm and for the book cover. Dave and Debbie Charlesworth deserve my thanks as well for their copy editing and suggestions that greatly improved the manuscript. For helping to pull this book together, correct my mistakes, and provide insightful suggestions, and for the many other tasks she performs so ably at SGG to help me focus my attention where it should be focused, I am grateful to Aubrie O'Brien.

My family deserves the most special praise. My wife Claudia encouraged (badgered?) me to write this book and has been most supportive of me and my ventures with Strategic Gaming. My son Alex came along when this book was started and I happily allowed him to interrupt its progress for more than 5 years. But he has also been an inspiration. Indeed, whenever he does things he should not, I am reminded of the essential art of making credible commitments. The final member of my immediate family is Nash, my dog. Nash is aptly named after game theorist and Nobel winner John Nash of *A Beautiful Mind* fame. His keen ability to signal his interests and influence me to take him on walks, and his unrelenting passion for playing games with the pesky squirrel in the backyard—with results that rival Wile E. Coyote's misadventures with the Roadrunner—are daily reminders of the universality and broad applicability of game theory.

–Paul Papayoanou, The Woodlands, Texas

# Publisher's Note

At the Orlando INFORMS conference, spring, 2010, Paul came up to me, introduced himself, and asked if we would have interest in publishing his book on game theory. I was immediately interested, as I had heard presentations on game theory at Chevron (where I work as a decision analyst or any other role that comes down the road) and I had heard good things about Paul and his company, SGG.

The first step was to read Paul's manuscript and dive into the material. As a result, I had a couple of reactions to Paul's book. First, Paul's writing is clear and he makes a complex topic easy to understand and interesting. Second, it seems to me that *decision analysis* is to *game theory* as *checkers* is to *chess*: game theory is a complex and challenging way of thinking. It can make a powerful addition to the analyst's tool box, but it isn't easy! You really have to *think* about this stuff–thank goodness for people like Paul who have figured out how to make it work and how to use it to add value in business situations.

Our goal in publishing this book is to provide an introduction for the practicing manager and his/her support staff concerning the powerful concepts of Strategic Gaming so that you can recognize situations where it can add value. Even though you probably won't be able to complete a full rigorous analysis yourself after reading the book, you should be able to (1) apply the concepts and the frameworks, and (2) recognize situations where an outside resource like Paul and SGG could help you add significantly to your bottom line.

Debbie and I are very grateful to Paul for seeking us out and pursuing this project. As Paul mentioned, thank you to Heather Reitze for a very attractive cover design. We also are thankful to the decision analysis community which has supported us in our DA and publishing endeavors, beginning with Tom Sciance, Conoco and SDG, leading to David Skinner, Gary Bush, the DSI gang, Bob Winkler, Pat Leach, DAAG, and now to Chevron (which recently won an INFORMS prize for DA implementation).

–Dave Charlesworth, Sugar Land, Texas

# Contents

## Part I: Game Theory and Strategic Gaming

## Part II: Primer

# Part I:
# Game Theory and
# Strategic Gaming

*"Man's mind, stretched to a new idea,*
*never goes back to its original dimensions."*
*– Oliver Wendell Holmes*

# 1

# Why Game Theory for Business

Business executives, managers, and negotiators regularly play games that are very similar to chess. They make decisions, their competitors and partners react, they make a counter response, and so on.

All savvy strategists and negotiators know that competitive actions and reactions matter, and they don't ignore them as they think through their strategic decisions and negotiation plans. How often, for instance, do we hear executives say that they want to find a "win-win" solution? Yet a serious, structured approach to potential action-reaction dynamics is seldom undertaken.

All too often, executives crafting strategies (or their highly paid consultants) neglect to carefully analyze the interdependence of their company's choices with those of other companies. There is little analysis of the potential downstream competitive implications that would be triggered by different strategic alternatives, and even less attention is paid to influencing the actions and reactions of others.

In other cases, executives who are quite rightly concerned about action-reaction dynamics find themselves spending inordinate amounts of time debating the merits of alternative strategic moves with their colleagues. Project team members usually wind up talking past one another in these meetings and all too often fail to reach internal alignment on a path forward. As a result, decisions get made too slowly, if at all, and the alignment essential for executing a strategy is often absent. Consequently, the upper hand is often yielded to more commercially savvy or well-positioned competitors.

None of this is surprising, for the "science" of business strategy that influences executives' and consultants' approaches has little to offer when it comes to analyzing complex action-reaction dynamics. This is the case for a whole host of strategic decisions, including:

- ♦ alliance and joint venture strategy,
- ♦ growth strategy,
- ♦ investment and capacity expansion decisions,
- ♦ pricing,
- ♦ market entry decisions,
- ♦ product launch timing,
- ♦ negotiations,
- ♦ licensing issues,
- ♦ political risk assessment and governmental relations, and
- ♦ auction design and bidding strategy.

While companies and their consultants often do sophisticated analyses to weigh alternative strategies for such issues, the studies all but ignore the potential moves and countermoves of others and what may be done to influence them.

For instance, some studies employ listing techniques to surface competitive issues. SWOT exercises, for example, involve detailing the specific strengths, weaknesses, opportunities, and threats a company faces. Michael Porter's Five Forces helps analysts understand the key aspects of competition in an industry: industry competitors, the threat of potential entrants, the bargaining power of suppliers, the bargaining power of buyers, and the threat of substitute products or services.[1] Both SWOT and Porter's Five Forces are useful first cuts and frameworks for analysis, but it is often unclear what to do with the lists they help generate. Indeed, it is typically not straightforward to use these lists to obtain the "answer" to a strategy question or to understand how companies can best influence others to shape the competitive terrain.

Other analyses incorporate interactive issues in only an ad hoc way. Some quantify a potential competitive action with a probability assessment that is often little more than a guess. Others altogether exclude the interactive dimension in their strategic analysis, saying that such matters are merely tactical and can be dealt with once the strategy is settled. However, the success or failure of a strategy may very well hinge on others' actions.

Strategy efforts thus tend to be at the 35,000-foot level, static in nature, and lacking in analysis of interactions with partners, competitors, and other stakeholders. And business strategies typically fail to consider how to best execute a strategy vis-à-vis these other stakeholders over time and under various contingencies.

Because these static, 35,000-foot strategies fail to map out actions, responses, and counter responses in a dynamic environment, companies can lock themselves into a strategy that does not enable adaptation to circumstances. Managers and negotiators may take short-sighted tactical decisions toward partners and competitors that fail to properly account for downstream implications or that are incompatible with the company's broader goals and strategy.

Seldom do strategy efforts develop explicit strategic and tactical plans that map out contingencies for how executives, managers, and negotiators should attempt to shape and then play the game of business as it unfolds. So while companies and their consultants regularly embark on ambitious strategy

---

(1) Michael E. Porter, *Competitive Strategy*.

efforts in the name of building long-term shareholder value, they often ignore or give short shrift to one of the most crucial determinants of value–action–reaction dynamics between competitors, partners, and other stakeholders. In turn, they fail to develop a robust, contingent plan of action that identifies when and how to influence others to ensure and enhance long-term value.

In short, business strategy is usually not very strategic, for it tends to neglect the all important interactive dimension. Rather, business strategy is often inward-looking, short-sighted, and reactive.

## Game Theory's Promise

One of the recipients of the 2005 Nobel Prize in Economic Sciences, Thomas Schelling, made similar arguments about international political-military strategy (e.g., nuclear deterrence) in his classic 1960 book, *The Strategy of Conflict*. In the first chapter, "The Retarded Science of International Strategy," Schelling discussed the grave dangers involved in not adopting an interactive approach to thinking about strategy and how game theory could help because of its focus on understanding how an individual's best course of action depends on his or her expectations of what others will do.[2]

In announcing the Nobel award, the Royal Swedish Academy of Sciences pointed to *The Strategy of Conflict* in particular as helping to make game theory "the dominant approach" to understanding conflict and cooperation in international affairs, economics, and throughout the social sciences.[3] Indeed, game theory is now widely considered in academia to be "the science of strategic thinking."[4]

Yet when it comes to the science and practice of business strategy, game theory has had little traction. Business strat-

---

(2) Thomas C. Schelling, *The Strategy of Conflict*.

(3) The Royal Swedish Academy of Sciences, "Press Release: The Bank of Sweden Prize in Economic Sciences in Memory of Alfred Nobel 2005," October 10, 2005.

(4) See Avinash K. Dixit and Barry J. Nalebuff, *Thinking Strategically: the competitive edge in business, politics, and everyday life*.

egy is much like international strategy was fifty years ago, when Schelling's path-breaking book was published.

This situation can and should be rectified. Game theory provides a logical and clear structure for looking at potential future interactions and helps predict and prescribe optimal strategic behavior. As such, game theory enables us to address a central question faced by all businesses at one time or another, if not regularly: Should we compete or cooperate, and how should we do so?

However, game theory, despite its name, is not necessarily about games with winners and losers. Nor is it a theory. It is a *tool* that helps us analyze situations in which two or more individuals' choices are interdependent, i.e., individuals' choices affect one another. Of central importance are situations in which the "players" are faced with dilemmas of competition and cooperation. In many cases, game theory provides insight into how players can achieve win-win outcomes by cooperating rather than competing. In other cases, game theory teaches us how to outmaneuver others or avoid being outmaneuvered.

## Nash's Contribution and Schelling's Adaptation

The applicability of game theory to situations beyond those with pure rivalry (and thus to a broad set of business issues) is due to John Nash's equilibrium concept. The contribution, which won Nash the Nobel Prize in Economics in 1994, enabled scholars to use game theory for analyzing a wide array of problems involving dilemmas of competition and cooperation rather than just win-lose situations.

In the Oscar-winning movie about Nash, *A Beautiful Mind*, the concept was explained with an intriguing bar scene. Nash, played by actor Russell Crowe, and some of his male graduate school friends were in the bar when five women walked in, one of them being a stunningly beautiful blonde. Nash's friends could not help but notice the blonde's entrance, and discussed how they would compete with one another to win her over. Nash was then supposedly inspired to his famous equilibrium, the subject of his Ph.D. dissertation at Princeton. Crowe's Nash told his friends that they should not approach the beautiful blonde, but instead agree to ask her friends to dance. "If we all go for the blonde, not one of us will get her," he argued. He reasoned that they would cancel one another out and so all would get turned down by the blonde. However, if they instead agreed to ask her friends to dance, they could all "win" by getting dates with the women. Cooperation could thus be better than competition.

While the story is fictional, it nicely illustrates how Nash's contribution transformed game theory from a narrow, zero-sum tool to a more general approach that could analyze competitive-cooperative dilemmas. Building on Nash's concept, Schelling made the compelling case that applications of game theory needed to go beyond zero-sum situations to focus on what he called "mixed-motive" or "bargaining" games, in which there is "a mix of mutual dependence and conflict, of partnership and competition." It is those types of games for which the Nash equilibrium is applicable and has much to offer.[5]

## Academia versus the Business World

These situations are also very common in the business world, where companies grapple with whether they should compete or cooperate with other companies. Yet game theory has not been widely applied in the development of business strategy because it has not been seen to be practical in the business world.

Game theory's success and evolution in academia may have actually hurt its applicability in the business world. Anyone who thumbs through the pages of a journal like *Econometrica* will quickly see that academics have made game theory an incredibly complex mathematical tool, even for the simplest of issues. For business executives, such complexity makes game theory daunting and impractical, for good rea-

---

(5) See *The Strategy of Conflict*, page 89.

son. Executives want tools that will help them cut through the complexity and make sense of it, not methods that make things more complex.

Conversely, game theory's applicability in business may also have been hurt by the exposure some have had to simple games like the famous Prisoner's Dilemma or Chicken (discussed in chapter 2). Such games provide interesting insights and suggest it would be valuable to think strategically, i.e., to think more carefully about the interdependence of choices with others. Yet business people exposed to such games do not know what more could really be done with game theory, other than to keep their simple but powerful lessons in mind. As one manager who learned about such games in a leading business school's executive education course commented to me, "I found game theory to be really interesting, but I didn't see how I could apply it."

While game theory is widely recognized in academia to be the leading tool for understanding the interdependence of choices, the issue is whether game theory can be a practical tool in the business world. Clearly game theory has changed widely held beliefs in economics, business, the law, the social sciences, and other academic disciplines. Since 1994 several scholars besides Nash and Schelling have received Nobel Prizes for their game-theoretic contributions.[6] Most of the top business schools now offer game theory courses and have game theorists on their faculty. Several books make the case

---

(6) In 1994, John Nash, the subject of the movie and Sylvia Nasar book, *A Beautiful Mind*, received the Nobel Prize in Economics along with Reinhard Selten and John Harsanyi. William Vickrey won the Nobel in 1996 for his pioneering work in incentives, asymmetric information, and auction theory. With Thomas Schelling, Robert Aumann won the 2005 Nobel for his game-theoretic work in repeated games. And most recently, Leonid Hurwicz, Eric Maskin and Roger Myerson won the 2007 Nobel prize for their work in mechanism design theory, a branch of game theory that extends the application of game theory to how different types of rules, or institutions, align individual incentives with overall social goals. Their work on allocation mechanisms has had a significant impact on the design of auctions, social welfare systems and many organizations.

that game theory should be used in business, as well as many other areas of life.[7]

Yet game theory has not been widely applied in the development of business strategy because it has not been seen to be practical and to have broad utility in the business world.[8] I have encountered many business people who have been exposed to game theory yet remain skeptical about its practicality. They comment that game theory:

♦ is too hard and complex to understand,
♦ is ambiguous as to how it can be applied,
♦ takes too long to do it right, or
♦ is unlikely to surface actionable insights of significant value.

These are reasonable concerns.

So can game theory, the science of strategic thinking, really make the practice of business strategy more sensible and better? That depends on whether it can efficiently generate insights that enable executives to better shape and play the game of business to capture substantial value. Strategic Gaming is a process for applying game theory that does just that.

## Game Theory for Business

By forcing a focus on the interdependence of choices between players in a practical way, Strategic Gaming helps make the science and practice of business strategy smarter. As such, it enables strategists and negotiators to efficiently and effectively tackle a wide range of business strategy questions in which competitive-cooperative dilemmas are a central

---

(7) See Adam M. Brandenburger and Barry J. Nalebuff, *Co-Opetition*, John McMillan, *Games, Strategies & Managers*, and Dixit and Nalebuff, *Thinking Strategically*.

(8) Schelling wrote in *The Strategy of Conflict*, page 10, that game theory had "been pitched at a level of abstraction where it has made little contact with the elements of a problem like deterrence." Something analogous can be said for business strategy.

concern, from deal making to competitive risk and partnering strategy.

Drawing on basic game theory principles and methods, Strategic Gaming helps executives, managers, and negotiators gain clarity about what the "game" that they are playing looks like, and how to best move and influence others at both the strategic and tactical level over time and across potential contingencies.

As will be demonstrated in subsequent chapters, Strategic Gaming is a straightforward and logical approach that provides high value insights quickly and efficiently. Strategists and negotiators who use Strategic Gaming are able to make sense of complex interactions and puzzling competitor behaviors, and find opportunities and commercial risks they had not seen previously. As they work through the process, evaluating the implications of a range of strategies and tactics, executives come away with a great capacity for shaping and playing "the game" to gain strategic advantages and avoid being blindsided by competitors, partners, suppliers, governments, and other players. Negotiators learn how to seal deals faster and capture maximum value, or walk away from talks that are doomed to fail.

In the chapters that follow, savvy strategists and negotiators of both large and small companies, in virtually any industry, will see that they can benefit greatly from Strategic Gaming. Conversely, it will be clear that ineffective strategizing vis-à-vis competitors, partners, and other stakeholders can be perilous to their company's fortunes. For their companies to survive and prosper, executives, managers, and negotiators must shape and play the game of business effectively. This book is a primer in how to do so.

*"Innovation is often a synthesis of art and science, and the best innovators often combine the two."*
*– Thomas Friedman*

# 2
# Overview of the Strategic Gaming Process

The first question I am usually asked is, "When should game theory be used?" Once there is an understanding of the potential areas of applicability, the question turns to, "How can game theory be applied effectively?" This chapter addresses both questions, for the Strategic Gaming process starts with diagnosis and then involves a three-stage approach for applying game theory in a practical and valuable way.

## When to Use Game Theory

Game theory is appropriate for business strategy when there is a need to gain insight into interactive situations with influence potential, i.e., when one's actions can affect the choices others will make, and vice versa. While an interdependence of choices is present in a wide range of interactive business situations, there are many business strategy questions for which game theory is not applicable. Just as it would be imprudent to use a hammer to nail in a screw, it would be inappropriate to apply game theory to some business problems. Diagnosis is thus of crucial importance.

For most business strategy questions, game theory and two other tools from the decision sciences—decision analysis and real options—are useful for framing and structuring problems, and for undertaking rigorous quantitative analysis. It is to these three capabilities that I typically focus the diagnosis.

Of these three tools, decision analysis is the most prominent and widely used in business. Its focus is evaluating big bet decisions in highly complex and uncertain situations. Real options (as applied to most business strategy problems) is a special case of decision analysis, focusing on how the choices we make today can affect the choices and information we have in the future. Real options analysis incorporates the value that comes from anticipated learning and the flexibility to take advantage of it through downstream decisions.[1]

Both decision analysis and real options typically use decision trees to map out a company's choices over time and key "chance event" uncertainties. Both are powerful methods for quantifying value and risk, comparing strategic alternatives, and systematically focusing teams on the factors that truly drive value.

As a third branch in the decision sciences, game theory has many similarities, but also some powerful differences. In decision trees, other players' moves are treated as uncertainties (though in practice they are often ignored altogether). Game trees, on the other hand, explicitly model other players' choices as decisions. Game theory requires consideration of the payoffs (value) to each of the players in the game tree, not just to one company, as is done in decision analysis and real options. For consulting assignments, my colleagues and I generally spend as much or more time understanding others' payoffs as we do our clients'. Meanwhile, all the chance

---

(1) Decision analysis texts include Robert T. Clemen, *Making Hard Decisions*, Second Edition, David C. Skinner, *Introduction to Decision Analysis*, Third Edition, and Peter McNamee and John Celona, *Decision Analysis for the Professional,* Third Edition. A useful resource on real options is Martha Amram and Nalin Kulatilaka, *Real Options: Managing Strategic Investment in an Uncertain World.*

*Figure 2.1: Decision Science Tools and their Applicability*

event uncertainties prominent in decision analysis and real options work can be incorporated into game trees and associated economic models.

As the three decision science approaches and tools are very useful for tackling a wide range of business strategy issues, I created a simple diagnostic to understand which is most appropriate. The diagnostic considers where issues fit along two broad dimensions—learning potential and influence issues. This yields a two-by-two matrix, shown in Figure 2.1, that has proven to be useful as prospective clients and I work together to understand the nature of their issues and the required analytics.

The first dimension, learning potential, concerns whether there can be a revelation of information upon which actions can then be taken. There is learning potential if we (or others) can make decisions, learn, and then make subsequent decisions based on that learning. If the situation is one with no significant uncertainties (apart from moves by other players) or we are faced with a big bet decision—we make a decision and then see what happens—there is no learning potential.

The second dimension is influence issues. Can we influence other players, or can they influence us? To determine this we need to first understand whether players' choices can impact the values other players receive from different strategy alternatives; if so, the players' choices are interdependent and contingent on the choices of others. That is the first condition. If that is true, we then need to ask if the actions we might take could affect the actions that others take, or vice versa. If so, influence issues exist. It is important to recognize that while the first condition may have been satisfied, the second may not. For example, what we buy or sell stocks for on the New York Stock Exchange depends on what others will sell or buy those stocks for, yet there are too many players for most of us to actually influence potential sellers or buyers. By contrast, in duopolistic or oligopolistic situations, the players typically have interdependent choices and can influence one another.

Figure 2.1 shows which tool is most appropriate for the different situations. In the lower left hand cell, there are no influence issues and no learning potential. In this case, traditional decision analysis is appropriate and very powerful. If we move up to the top left cell, where there can be learning but influence issues are not important, a real options frame and evaluation is best.[2]

For example, oil and gas companies pay millions of dollars for seismic studies to determine whether it makes sense to drill a much more expensive exploratory well. If they drill a successful exploratory well, that will help them decide whether to drill one or more appraisal wells. In turn, those will affect their options for development of the field.[3] Similarly, pharmaceutical companies considering development of early

(2) Amram and Kulatilaka, *Real Options,* page 24 cite five situations in which a real options analysis is needed. All five involve learning and the ability to make future decisions after learning.

(3) Oil companies typically treat such issues with a Value of Information (VOI) approach whereby a determination is made as to the value of further drilling. That is not necessarily a bad thing, for the contingent investment decisions are not far off in the future. If, however, a strategy contained the potential for learning from a well far into the future, this should entail real options thinking.

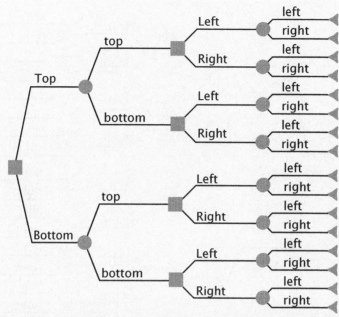

Decision nodes are squares. Chance nodes, which represent competitor decisions in this case, are circles.

*Figure 2.2: Decision Tree of a Game Between Two Players*

stage drugs should think about their investment decisions with a real options frame, for a number of uncertainties about future trials and FDA approval will be involved in assessing the value of decisions that impact subsequent decisions and value far into the future. In both examples, companies are paying to learn, at each stage, about whether and how they should exercise future options. Since they have the potential for choosing options that facilitate learning, real options is the best frame for analysis.

Game theory is most appropriate in the two right hand cells. In these, one or more players can influence others, and this interactive dynamic is captured by game theory better than it is by decision analysis or real options. Decision trees used in decision analysis and real options cannot model moves by other players in a tractable or sensible fashion. Decision trees require that we assign probabilities at every possible node for moves by other players (as shown in Figure 2.2),

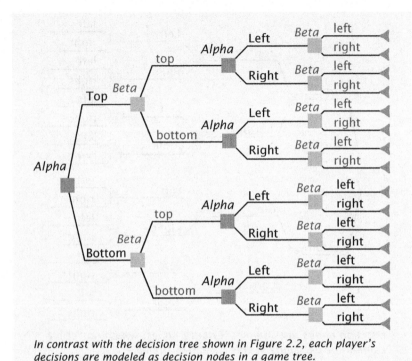

*In contrast with the decision tree shown in Figure 2.2, each player's decisions are modeled as decision nodes in a game tree.*

*Figure 2.3: Game Tree of a Game Between Two Players*

which can easily lead to a highly subjective and arduous process. Moreover, doing so encodes what we know or imagine today, and so it blocks our ability to learn anything from analysis about others' motivations and incentives. Also, assigning probabilities to others' moves is inconsistent with the action-reaction, chess-type of logic that businesses are actually engaged in (or should be in) when determining what the best course of action is. Game trees, by contrast, treat all players' decisions as choices (as illustrated by Figure 2.3). The need to assign probabilities is obviated and the resulting analysis entails more realistic action-reaction logic.

One might ask, "What about uncertainties involving big bets and options? Can game theory incorporate those as well as the interactive dynamic?" Yes, game trees can model all the uncertainties we find in decision trees, while treating all players' choices as decisions. A game tree is thus a more general tool than is a decision tree; game theory is most appropriate

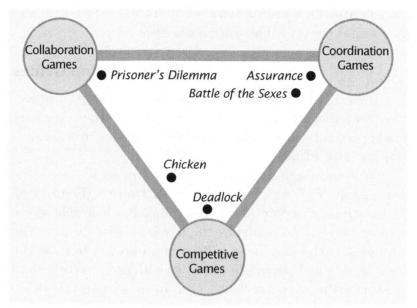

*Figure 2.4: The "3Cs" of Game Situations*

whenever there are influence issues, regardless of the nature of the uncertainties.

## The 3Cs

When a situation appears to have influence issues, it is useful to identify the key game dilemmas across three dimensions I refer to as the "3Cs." The 3Cs refer to three types of game situations, and all games fit somewhere within the 3C space illustrated in Figure 2.4.

Identifying where in the 3C space a company and other players are, and what outcomes are possible, serves as a transition from diagnosis to the Strategic Gaming process. It helps us gain a sense of how difficult the issues are and the value at stake in the game. (If little is at stake, game analysis is probably not warranted.) It also helps frame and structure the business problem by providing a better understanding of the key questions to address.

The top of the diagram represents cooperative games and the bottom of the triangle refers to competitive games. Cooperative games come in two forms—ones in which there is the potential for coordination and others where formal agreements that ensure collaboration are necessary.

## Coordination Games

Coordination games require no more than a verbal agreement for a cooperative outcome to be realized. There is a win-win opportunity, and deviating from the agreement will result in a lose-lose situation.

To illustrate this idea, consider the famous Battle-of-the-Sexes game. The game is set up as a 2 x 2 matrix (Figure 2.5). In this simple coordination game a couple has to decide where to go out on Saturday night—the movies or the theater. The man prefers the movies and the woman prefers to go to the theater, though both would rather go with their partner than go alone to the movies or the theater. In the matrix, this situation is represented with numbers, where the man and woman get 2 for going on a date at their more preferred destination, a 1 for going on a date to their less preferred destination, and 0 if they go alone to either destination.[4] In this game, the two obviously need to coordinate on whether to go to the movies or the theater. Perhaps they will agree to go to the movies one week and the theater the following week. Or maybe one will insist on the movies or the theater and the other will feel impelled to go along to reach a win-win, even though it's not his or her most preferred outcome.

In business, we see similarly obvious win-wins when there are questions about the terms on which the parties can reach agreement. One player may be positioned to win more than the other, or they may strike a compromise deal that balances interests just as the man and woman in the game could agree to alternate movie and theater dates on subsequent weeks. As long as expectations and perceptions converge around the

---

(4) One could argue that the man would prefer going to the movies alone over the theater alone, and the woman would prefer the theater alone over the movies alone. That would make the zeros in the top right and bottom left cells different numbers. However, those numbers would still be smaller than the date outcomes, so they would not change the outcome and the need for coordination.

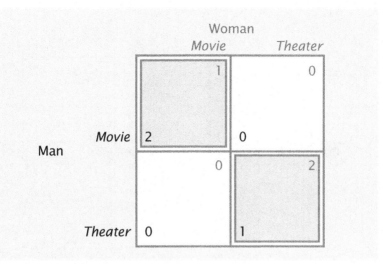

*Figure 2.5: Battle of the Sexes*

notion that a win-win can be coordinated, the question of cooperation is typically not if, but when and how.

## Collaboration Games

Collaboration games are characterized by the possibility of a win-win, but also an incentive to deviate from an agreement to gain an advantage. Such games are the reason we have legally binding contracts, which ensure that each party to a contract lives up to its side of an agreement. Without such an enforcement mechanism, each would have an incentive to deviate from the agreement. Knowing that, the parties would fail to reach an agreement and not realize a win-win outcome.

The famous Prisoner's Dilemma game is the classic example for this common situation. In the original story behind the game, two criminals are captured and placed in separate rooms where they are asked to turn states' evidence on one another. If neither finks on the other, the District Attorney will only be able to put each away for one year on minor charges. So the District Attorney makes an offer to each. If only one finks on his accomplice, the one who finked will go free while

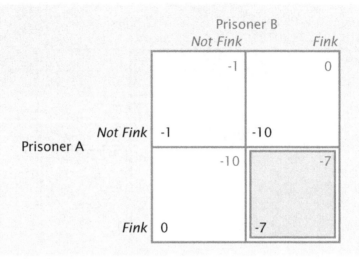

*Figure 2.6: Prisoner's Dilemma*

the other will be put away for 10 years. If both fink on each other, they will each get 7 year sentences. The game and this payoff structure (with years in prison as negative numbers) are shown in Figure 2.6.

We can see that the District Attorney's offer creates an incentive for each to fink on the other, for each can gain from finking on the other and lose if the other finks on him. The outcome in which both fink on the other, though suboptimal for both prisoners, is thus the logical conclusion (and the Nash equilibrium, a game-theoretic concept I will discuss in chapter 4). If they both could trust one another to not fink, each would get off with much lighter sentences, just one year each. But the incentive structure created by the District Attorney makes trust impossible. Each has an incentive to fink on the other to go free and avoid the worst possible jail sentence (the "sucker's payoff") and since both have that incentive, they each wind up with 7 year prison terms.

The Prisoner's Dilemma is seen to have broad applicability in and outside the business world. Besides being the basis for most contracts, some would say this can explain price wars, why companies might lack the trust necessary to forge a strategic alliance, or why two or more companies may decide a formal joint venture to ensure cooperation is in order. Unions are another example of how the Prisoner's Dilemma can be transcended. If workers can avoid paying membership dues but gain the benefits of a union negotiating better salary and benefits packages, they would shirk paying them. Yet, if all workers did so, the union would cease to exist. Hence, unions lobby for laws that mandate all workers in a union shop pay dues.

## Competitive Games

Competitive games are characterized by situations in which players have an incentive to win and a cooperative outcome is either unattractive or not possible. They are not necessarily the same as zero-sum games, for there is not necessarily a winner and a loser—it is possible to see lose-lose outcomes or ties.

The famous game of Chicken, shown in Figure 2.7, is one such competitive game. The story behind this game is that two teenagers with their muscle cars dare each other to a game of nerves. Each will drive at the other, and the first to swerve loses the game. Of course, if neither swerves, they will crash into each other and, at minimum, destroy their beloved cars. If they both swerve, the game is a draw—no one has bragging rights.[5]

The key to such games is in finding a way to move first or make a credible commitment. For example, if one of the teenagers could pull the steering wheel off the column of his car and hold it out the window for his competitor to see, he will have made a credible commitment to not swerve. His competitor would be impelled to swerve and avoid mutual disaster.

In real-life business situations, Chicken-like games are quite common. Labor strikes and labor-management negotiations are often a test of resolve – which side will blink

---

(5) The size of the numbers shown in the matrix doesn't matter to the story behind this game. What matters is the order in which they appear. Thus, crashing into each other might be much worse than -10 to the players, but all that matters is that this be the mutually worst outcome. This will be discussed more in chapter 4.

|  | Person B | |
|---|---|---|
|  | *Swerve* | *Don't Swerve* |
| *Swerve* | 5       5 | 10       2 |
| *Don't Swerve* | 2       10 | -10       -10 |

*Figure 2.7: Chicken*

first? Will labor end its strike and come back to work, or will management make concessions to end the strike and resume business? In other situations, a company may make a public commitment to enter a particular market, and if that commitment is sufficiently credible, a competitor can be successfully deterred from entering as well. In other business situations, two companies may realize they are headed for mutual disaster and find a compromise to avert that outcome. More often than not, though, they will try to outmaneuver one another.

Another competitive game is Deadlock, shown in Figure 2.8. In this game, each of the players has a dominant strategy to defect since they would get 4 or 3, the two best payoffs regardless of what the other does. There is no room for cooperation or compromise.

We find such situations in industries and situations where competition is clearly the only option, and the question is merely about how. In the pharmaceutical industry, for example, large, integrated companies seldom cooperate with one another. Instead, they race to market with their drugs and seek to differentiate them from those of their rivals. Cooperation may happen when one company's sales force has

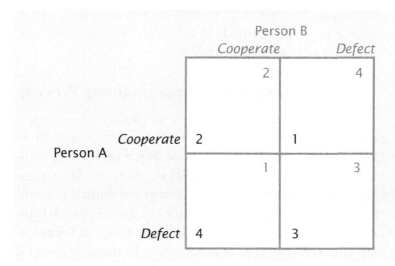

*Figure 2.8: Deadlock*

a significant advantage in a particular region or when two drugs can compete more effectively as a combination, but such instances are not common.

By contrast, oil and gas companies seldom pursue large exploration and production projects that cost billions of dollars without partners. Typically they form joint ventures with other companies to help finance the projects and reduce risk exposure. But unlike drugs in the pharmaceutical industry, oil and gas are commodities. Differentiation is not important, so there is more room for cooperation.

In the real world, few issues I come across fit perfectly in one corner of the 3C triangle. Indeed, I have found it is dangerous to assess a situation and simply say that it is a Prisoner's Dilemma, Chicken game or something else. There are typically elements of one or more of the dilemmas we find in such games, so it is important to structure the game methodically, in ways I will demonstrate in the rest of this chapter and in chapter 3. Thinking about these archetypes is part of a background assessment that supports the more methodical approach, but it does not replace it. Forcing real world problems into a single archetype may lead to an over-simplification or mischaracterization of the situation and serious errors in how to approach it.

## Overview of the Strategic Gaming Process

Strategic Gaming is an efficient methodology for applying game theory effectively. It addresses five basic questions drawn from game theory, which underpin a three-stage process of Dynamic Framing, Strategy Evaluation, and Execution Planning. The approach is straightforward and intuitive, and produces highly valuable insights quickly. In the end, Strategic Gaming helps companies develop a dynamic road map—a strategic and tactical plan of action to help them shape and play the game effectively under all feasible contingencies.

## Five Questions

When I first developed Strategic Gaming, I thought back to why I became enamored with game theory in graduate school at UCLA. To me, game theory had a simple, elegant structure that provided very powerful insights with a small amount of information. I realized that any game-theoretic model requires addressing just five basic questions:

1. Who are the key players?
2. What choices do they have?
3. In what sequence do they make these choices?
4. What are the key uncertainties?
5. What are the payoffs to each player for each possible outcome?

I have not seen these five questions in any game theory text, or anywhere else. Nonetheless, they are the core of game theory models and the key to making game theory practical in the business world. Hence, they are at the heart of the Strategic Gaming process.

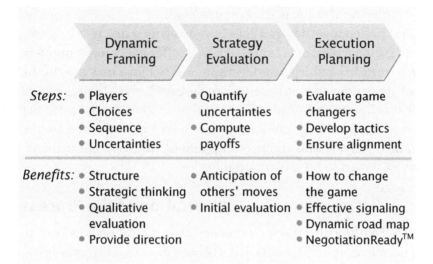

| | Dynamic Framing | Strategy Evaluation | Execution Planning |
|---|---|---|---|
| *Steps:* | • Players<br>• Choices<br>• Sequence<br>• Uncertainties | • Quantify<br>  uncertainties<br>• Compute<br>  payoffs | • Evaluate game<br>  changers<br>• Develop tactics<br>• Ensure alignment |
| *Benefits:* | • Structure<br>• Strategic thinking<br>• Qualitative<br>  evaluation<br>• Provide direction | • Anticipation of<br>  others' moves<br>• Initial evaluation | • How to change<br>  the game<br>• Effective signaling<br>• Dynamic road map<br>• NegotiationReady™ |

*Figure 2.9: The Strategic Gaming Process*

## Three Stages

As colleagues and I refined Strategic Gaming, three distinct stages of the process emerged. Each has particular steps and benefits that are summarized in Figure 2.9.

First there is Dynamic Framing, a stage for framing (or scoping) and structuring situations. Here the first four questions are addressed, and doing so enables the construction of game trees. Game trees map out the players' possible choices, in sequence, as well as key uncertainties. This provides much-needed structure. Also, building game trees helps people put themselves into the shoes and minds of other key players better, which enhances strategic thinking. Some qualitative evaluation is done here as well, which helps to focus subsequent analysis and can provide useful insights and direction for short-term actions.

Second is Strategy Evaluation, a stage for quantitatively evaluating game trees. The fifth question, about payoffs, comes into play here. Decision analysis methods are typically used for modeling payoffs (values) and then game theory techniques for solving and analyzing games are employed to gain insights and understand which strategies are best given key uncertainties and the likely moves and countermoves of other players.

The final stage is Execution Planning. Here all the analysis is pulled together and goes beyond strict game tree analysis to develop a plan of action that can be effectively implemented. We want to be able to understand how to move now and in the future, under various contingencies, and what tactics would best influence other players. Although tactical moves are not typically part of game trees, tactics will be informed by the game analysis and should complement the strategic alternatives shown to be most valuable.

## Illustration of the Process

To illustrate the methodology at work, let us now turn to a case example. The case (like others discussed in this book) is disguised. It involves a client I will call Nash Energy. Nash was a small alternative energy startup that went into business before it was stylish to be in the green business. Nash's CEO saw that his company was in a fragmented segment of the alternative energy industry and that consolidation was inevitable. There were competing technologies and no player had significant scale. As such, every competitor faced low margins and volumes. There was also significant public policy uncertainty over if, how, and when regulations would help the industry grow, although the potential was seen as substantial.

The question Nash's CEO had was, "How can Nash Energy capitalize on the inevitable consolidation of the industry?" Given the need to understand potential action-reaction dynamics, Nash's CEO saw that Strategic Gaming could provide the insight he sought.

The Dynamic Framing part of the process involves addressing the first four questions. Meeting with the CEO and his key people, I was able to complete this part of the process in about three hours. The Nash team initially identified ten potential players, but after considering player choices, four (including Nash) were seen to be key players.

Choices in the game broke down quite simply between offers to cooperate in strategic alliances, acceptance or rejec-

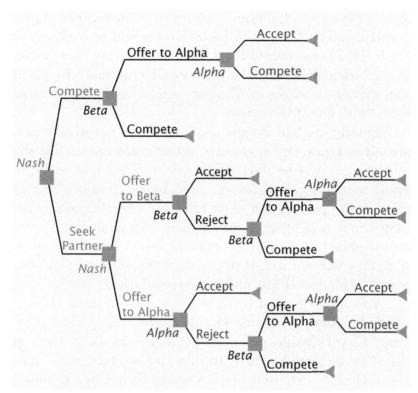

*Figure 2.10: Nash Energy Example Game Tree*

tion of such offers, and competitive (or, go-it-alone) strategies. These are illustrated by the game tree in Figure 2.10, which shows the alternatives for Nash and two other players in the game. (Not shown here is the fourth key player. Nash was already in negotiations with that player, and that was modeled as well, for we wanted to know at what point Nash should seal a deal or walk away. For simplicity, though, I have left that player out of the tree shown here.)

Although the game tree shows a sequence of moves between Nash, Alpha, and Beta, this could be different—perhaps Alpha and Beta would form an alliance before Nash makes an offer. There is not necessarily a correct sequence. However, it is important to start with something, and by doing so we could easily see that moving first could be advantageous, while waiting might be dangerous. The game tree helped the team see that if they did not quickly seal the deal with the fourth player, Delta, and then make a deal with Alpha, then Alpha and Beta might form an alliance that would be a threat to Nash. Time was seen to be of the essence. This short-term, qualitative insight was later confirmed by the analysis, which also showed us where and how we might be willing to make a deal with one of those two.

Finally, we had to take account of uncertainties, which are of two types. One is chance events: outcomes outside the control of any player and that no player can know in advance. These uncertainties can be revealed during the game so that one or more players can move after the uncertain event becomes known, or after all moves have been made (i.e., downstream uncertainties). In this case, all chance events identified were downstream uncertainties, and included market size, potential market share, and future regulations.

The other type of uncertainty is private information, which has to do with uncertainty players have about how other players value potential outcomes in the game and thus how they might move. In this case, we recognized that ally reliability (whether players would be inclined to follow through on their side of the bargain in a strategic alliance) was potentially important. Private information issues may make some players reluctant to forge alliances with another player, or alliances that do form may be less than are hoped for due to some defection by one of the players. Hence, we identified private information as potentially important, and would work to quantify this in the next stage of the process, Strategy Evaluation.

With our game tree structure, the payoffs to each of the players in the game could then be modeled in a straightforward way. The game showed five possible outcomes:

- ♦ No alliances (everyone goes it alone),
- ♦ A Nash-Delta alliance only,
- ♦ A Nash-Delta alliance and an Alpha-Beta alliance,
- ♦ A Nash-Delta and Nash-Alpha alliance, or
- ♦ An Alpha-Beta alliance only.

Reasonable assessments were made about market size, share,

and profit margin for these different scenarios. These are not factors we can know with certainty; in fact, they are downstream uncertainties. Hence, the modeling needed to also provide an uncertainty range for such parameters in order to do a robust analysis.

Where strategic alliances were involved, assumptions were made about the profit-sharing terms between the players. These could easily be (and were) modified to analyze the effects of different possible terms on player strategies.

After some initial analysis that assumed perfect reliability, we incorporated private information uncertainty to see how that could affect outcomes. This involved some assessments about how reliable the different players would appear to one another.

With the economic model, we could then populate our game tree with payoffs for each of the players. We found:

(1) the deal with Delta was an obvious win-win, and

(2) the initial insight from Dynamic Framing that time was of the essence regarding a deal with Alpha was correct.

The game tree analysis revealed that there was an incentive for Alpha and Beta to forge a strategic alliance. As Figure 2.11 shows, accepting an offer from Nash would net Alpha a payoff of 160, while making a deal with Beta has a payoff of 200. Hence, Nash needed to make its deal with Delta and then try to secure one with Alpha. Since the Delta deal (not shown in the tree) was far less important than getting Alpha to be a strategic ally, thus avoiding an Alpha-Beta alliance, it was imperative to move quickly, even if that meant leaving some value on the table with Delta. It also meant that Nash might have to sweeten the deal to Alpha so that Alpha could get a payoff greater than 200. Transferring 40 or more in value to Alpha would mean a smaller payoff to Nash, 380 or less, but that would still be substantially better than the 190 Nash would get in facing an Alpha-Beta alliance.

Another route Nash could take to securing an alliance with Alpha was to exploit potential concerns Alpha might

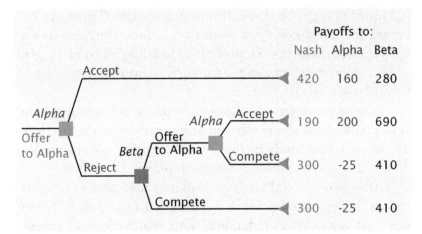

*Figure 2.11: Key Subgame of Nash Energy Example*

have about ally reliability. When we included the significant potential for Beta to be an unreliable partner and Nash's relative reliability, the game analysis showed quantitatively that Nash was a more attractive partner to Alpha than Beta would be. Nash therefore needed to play up this issue in discussions with Alpha, and doing so might mean that there would not need to be term concessions.

The picture was thus quite clear for the Execution Planning stage. Still, it was important to think through any potential game changers and lay out clearly what the strategic and tactical road map should be in order to execute the action plan. With the transparency of the analysis and conversations that enabled full ownership of the results by the CEO, this was quite straightforward for Nash.

As shown in Figure 2.12, Nash was going to work to quickly seal the deal with Delta, even if that meant leaving some value on the table, and then approach Alpha with a strategic alliance offer. If Nash appeared to be failing to sway Alpha, it could then sweeten the offer, knowing that approximately 40 in value should be sufficient to secure an alliance with Alpha. Above that amount, Nash should be stubborn. Although the analysis shows that Nash could concede more, it also had pointed to the importance of ally reliability, and how Beta's unreliability could make Beta an unattractive alliance

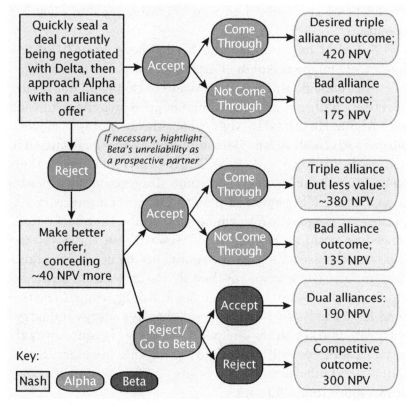

*Figure 2.12: Nash Energy Dynamic Road Map*

partner for Alpha. In fact, when discussing this with Nash's CEO, he looked me straight in the eye and said, "I know exactly what I will tell them, and I won't offer them any more." The analysis had given him the insight and confidence he needed to proceed. He would make a strong effort to employ this tactic, highlighting Beta's recent unreliable behavior in the industry, before considering sweetened offers.

In more complicated projects, the dynamic road map will typically be more complex and detailed, and may include tasks for more than one business unit to make sure that there is coordination within an organization. Whatever the case, the dynamic road map may and should vary on a case-by-case basis. It needs to lay out a contingent plan of action that should be of sufficient depth and detail to enable effective execution.

So, what happened in the Nash Energy case? Did the Nash CEO follow the plan of action and was it successful?

Sure enough, the Nash CEO went to Delta and finalized a deal there within a week, and then hopped on a plane to visit with Alpha. He talked to Alpha about the advantages of partnering with Nash versus Beta, and Alpha quickly admitted it had no desire to go with Beta. Nash's CEO knew right then he had the upper hand. Negotiations dragged on for a month or so, but the CEO stood firm on the terms of an agreement. In the end, he got the agreement with Alpha that he wanted, conceding nothing. He told me afterward that the Strategic Gaming exercise gave him the confidence he needed to stand firm and not leave value on the table. And with its strategic alliances with Delta and Alpha, Nash Energy came to be the clear leader in its segment of the alternative energy industry, with 75% market share and nearly 20 times revenue growth in two years, as well as a highly profitable business. Since that critical juncture in Nash Energy's life, the company has grown more than 300 times.

I now turn, in the next three chapters, to a detailed primer for each stage of the process. For readers not interested in being practitioners, this will likely be more detail than they are interested in. Those readers can safely skim through to Chapters 6, 7, and 8, which provide case examples and to Chapter 9, which discusses why and how Strategic Gaming should be applied to project work and integrated into strategy processes to tackle dilemmas of competition and cooperation practically and with high value benefits.

# Part II: Primer

*"See the whole board."*
*– Actor Martin Sheen as President Josiah Bartlet on*
The West Wing *television show, making a reference*
*to chess in discussing with an aide how to think*
*about options and potential responses in a fictional*
*crisis in the Taiwan Straits.*

# 3

# Dynamic Framing

Dynamic Framing involves scoping the critical business issues and structuring the interactions and key uncertainties that comprise the game. This is essential to understanding what the competitive landscape looks like and to seeing how we and other players *could* move, much as we would try to do in playing a game of chess. This lays the foundation for the second stage of the process, Strategy Evaluation, as it provides crucial guidance for the economic modeling that underpins game analysis.

Although determining which moves are best is typically left to the evaluation (so that our insights are rigorously grounded in quantitative measures), we are usually able to draw out important qualitative insights during the Dynamic Framing phase that provide short-term strategic and tactical direction.

## Background Assessment and Scoping

As discussed in the previous chapter, Dynamic Framing requires that four questions drawn from game theory be addressed. However, before doing so it is important to do a background business assessment. Without a general understanding of the history and basic issues, it is impossible to think sensibly about how one might scope and structure the game.

Business assessment typically has three components:

(1) Data analysis and review,

(2) Interviews, and

(3) Key issues and dilemmas.

First is a basic data analysis and review. Start by reviewing all written materials on the issues—work to date, presentations, information from third party sources, and whatever else may be important. This need not be a detailed reading of everything. In fact, that would probably be counterproductive as one can easily get mired in details. Rather, it should be enough to have a basic understanding of the competitive landscape and potential issues.

Second, interview as many people who have a direct or indirect interest in the project, or who otherwise can provide expert knowledge, as is feasible. In those interviews we want to collect information and hear interviewees' perspectives on what they believe the key issues are. This is important since it is ultimately crucial to gain internal alignment with a team and management. Without entertaining all viewpoints, that is all but impossible.

The interviews and review of written materials should focus on:

♦ the key players,

♦ the basic choices that the client and other key players may have,

♦ steps that have already been taken to think through the issues, and

♦ the prospective benefits and risks to the players.

We should not be after details at this point, but rather a high level overview. The goal is to understand the appropriate scope of the project and to have sufficient background to know how to help a project team structure the game effectively.

The third part of business assessment is to use what is learned from the interviews and written materials to hone in on the key issues and game dilemmas. Here the 3Cs triangle discussed in chapter 2 is quite useful. By taking from what we have learned and thinking about where in the diagram the situation seems to be, and where it could go and why, we will begin to gain clarity about how to scope and structure the game. Indeed, in many cases we will be able to group potential choices into collaboration, coordination, and competition buckets, thus helping us to map out the game effectively.

In doing the business assessment it is important to avoid a narrow definition of the issues to address. All too often I see project teams develop too narrow a scope; in most cases this seems to provide a level of comfort to the analysis, a way to provide an adequate answer. Such thinking is usually misguided, especially if other players are involved. Without taking a sufficiently broad scope, we can miss potentially important factors and could more easily find ourselves blindsided unnecessarily. This is not to say we should include everything in our scope; we should not try to "solve world hunger." We should, though, have a scope that probably takes us outside our comfort zone. Doing so often surfaces important issues and clarifies the situation. We can always refine and limit that scope later—and we usually do—but if we start with a narrow frame it is very difficult to recognize when a broader scope is needed.

Armed with the background assessment, it is now possible to address the four framing questions drawn from game theory:

(1) Who are the key players?
(2) What choices do they have?
(3) In what sequence do they make these choices?
(4) What are the key uncertainties?

# Players

Identifying potential key players is the first step. However, our initial list of key players may not be the ultimate assessment. In fact, *who the key players really are* is one of the insights we get from a Strategic Gaming exercise. For instance, in the Nash Energy project discussed in chapter 2, the client team listed ten players. As we worked through the process, only four including the client were found to be important. This important insight was reached in just a couple hours. As we worked through the evaluation, we quickly found that the situation with one of the four companies was very straightforward, and so the analysis narrowed to just three companies (including Nash Energy).

Similarly, in an engagement with an oil and gas company, five players were identified, but the analysis led us to focus on the client and the biggest partner. The other three partners in the oil field, we found, would likely be followers and would not independently influence the two most significant players. This finding in itself was an important intuition, and one that ran counter to what the client team had believed.

Knowing that our view of who the key players are may change as we learn from the game analysis, what players should go on our initial list? What exactly do we mean by *key players*?

*Key players* are those whose choices may have a significant effect on the outcome of the game, who have a stake in that outcome, and who are not impartial. This will typically include partners, competitors, suppliers or buyers, and governments who are making impactful choices.

Others we may be tempted to think of as players are typically not considered key players. Judges and juries, for example, will have some biases but are largely impartial and do not have a personal stake in the outcome (at least, they should not). The same can often be said of government regulatory agencies such as the FERC, the FDA, or the Interstate Commerce Commission. While the decisions of judges, juries, and regulatory agencies may have a substantial impact on a game's outcome, we would not consider them players given that they are somewhat impartial arbiters who do not have a stake in the outcome. That said, we can and often should model their decisions as chance event uncertainties—there is some probability they will rule one way, and some chance another way—as we would do in a decision analysis exercise.

One might object to this, saying that a company using Strategic Gaming will have an interest and ability to influence these people or entities. That is true, but influence is around providing and shaping information to influence a perspective rather than the interests of the judge, jury, or governmental agency. For instance, in one project the team and I recognized that the rules that would be set up by a regulatory agency were a key uncertainty as to how the client would fare. We treated that agency's decision on the rules as a chance event, but then considered the implications of different rules for the game. Understanding those implications, we then had a clear sense of what we should inform and ask the government agency about, as well as what to request, in implementing the strategy. Thus, the agency's decision was treated as a chance event in the game tree analysis, but we developed an execution plan that considered what tactics could best influence that agency's perspective on the issues.

There is one other case in which we would treat a player's move as a chance event. If a player's move has little to do with the game being modeled and more to do with other factors, it is usually best to think of that move as a chance event. For instance, in an oil and gas project the team was concerned about whether its partner would decide against renewing their joint venture. That decision could affect how my client could play the game. However, the partner was likely to make the decision independently of the particular matter at hand since the joint venture covered many assets, not just the asset under consideration. Hence, we modeled the partner's decision as a chance event at the beginning of the game, looking then at the scenarios with and without the partner.[1]

Apart from governmental regulatory agencies, I have found that governments should usually be considered players, for they may be greatly concerned about tax revenues, jobs, resource conservation, or something else. They also play an active role in negotiating with, and seeking to influence, companies doing business within their borders, and vice versa. And in thinking about governments as players, it is often important to disaggregate governments to be clear about which official or branch of government is important and what their specific interests are. After all, governments are composed of varied and often conflicting interests.

In thinking about the key players, we also need to consider the number of players that can be incorporated into a Strategic Gaming exercise. Typically, five players are the maximum. This is because the value of Strategic Gaming lies in the insight it provides into how to best influence others. If there are a large number of players, influence becomes difficult. For example, the stock market is a game—how much those who play the market earn or lose on particular stocks depends on how much others will pay for or sell those stocks. However, it is very difficult to influence a sufficient number of players to markedly change a stock price in one's favor. There are exceptions, but such efforts are usually unethical or illegal (Enron's inflation of its stock price with accounting improprieties, for example). Since the ability to influence is minimal, we would not use Strategic Gaming to understand how to play the stock market.

---

(1) Interestingly, this analysis showed that it would be beneficial to not have the partner. Hence, one interesting outcome of the project was the client's realization that it could choose not to renew the joint venture, an option that had not been considered seriously. The client had been in reactive mode, waiting to see what the partner would do. Yet for playing the game being modeled, we found it would be highly beneficial to not have the partner. This finding was a catalyst behind serious discussions within the organization about the usefulness of the joint venture in other areas, and whether the relationship should be renewed.

The five-player limit is not a hard and fast rule though. In some cases, it may make sense to combine and group similar, like-minded players, in which case quite a few players may be "in the game." In other cases, we will find that as we map out games, only two or three players are really involved in parts of the game (what we call subgames), even if there are a number of others in the larger game. Isolating subgames for analysis is often very important, so setting an arbitrary limit of five may wrongly dissuade one from using Strategic Gaming or may constrain the frame for analysis unnecessarily.

Another consideration is that Strategic Gaming analysis often helps narrow down the number of key players so that we can focus on the most important stakeholders. If we find that the number of key players nonetheless remains large and that a game-theoretic analysis will be intractable, we can easily shift to a decision analytic or real options framework.

For such reasons, I prefer to start broadly, and then narrow down as necessary and appropriate to complete the analysis. This ensures an appropriate scope and a structure that does not leave crucial factors out of the analysis. Such breadth is not only important in identifying key players, but also in looking at players' possible choices, to which we now turn.

## Choices and Sequence

Once the key players are identified, we consider what choices those players may have and the sequence (or simultaneity) in which they are likely to make those choices.

I typically address these two questions simultaneously, and I usually use game trees to facilitate this part of the framing process. Game trees look a lot like decision trees. However, unlike decision trees, *each* player's moves in a game tree are modeled as decisions (square nodes), not as chance event uncertainties (circle nodes). This contrast with decision trees was shown in Figures 2.2 and 2.3 of the previous chapter.

Note that chance event uncertainties can also be present in game trees. This is illustrated in Figure 3.1, a game tree

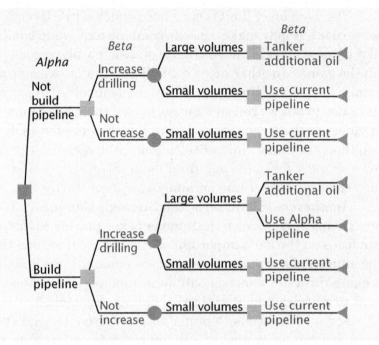

*Figure 3.1: Game Tree with Chance Events*

that shows each player's moves treated as decisions, with the uncertainty about the size of oil volumes represented as a chance event. In this game tree, Alpha can build a pipeline, creating a potentially valuable option for shipping large volumes of oil and gas. But whether this option will be beneficial depends on whether Beta decides to increase drilling and the chance event in the tree, the size of volumes.

Treating other players' decisions as choices rather than uncertainties has both technical and practical benefits. Because we do not have to assign numerous probabilities to solve the game, we can identify quite a few choices for each player over time. This means we can be much more liberal about what we model than we could be with decision analysis or real options approaches. Game theory thus enables the structuring of complex action-reaction dynamics with game trees.

An implication of using game trees is that a project team will become more capable of objectively understanding other players' positions and viewpoints. This is because we never ask what a player will do, how a player ranks his or her choices, or with what probability a player will move one way or another. Instead we ask what choices a player has at a particular point in the game tree. As we will see later, quantification will help determine how players should decide. Taking this approach enables us to objectively determine, and sharply reduce our uncertainty about, how other players should move so we can identify, in turn, our best strategies and tactics.

In thinking broadly about players' possible choices (rather than likely actions), we will also open up the frame substantially. Indeed, my experience in constructing game trees with project teams is that blinders come off and light bulbs start to click on. Team members start to realize both commercial risks not previously recognized and opportunities for gaining strategic advantages. Moreover, by identifying potential choices, executives do not jump to conclusions about what others will do and instead have an open mind about the possibilities.

In sketching out the choices that we and others have, it is very useful to be methodical. If feasible, I prefer to ask about one decision at a time. I may start out asking what choices we have at the start of the game and label branches of a game tree accordingly. Then, we would consider one of those branches and ask what choices our competitor has after we make that particular choice. We would, at that point, identify the potential choices (again, *not* how the competitor will likely move), and label branches accordingly. We would then take one of the competitor's choice branches and ask what choices we or another player have at that point. The process continues in this way, one branch at a time.

While this may seem like a tedious process, it is not. It is a methodical yet creative way of broadening a team's understanding of the issues. Feedback from project teams is that this process is not boring. In fact, teams are typically energized and remark at how eye-opening the process is. They talk about how it helps them to recognize possibilities for themselves and for others, how they see new avenues for creating value, and how it helps them avoid getting blindsided by others' "surprising" actions.

As you no doubt can surmise, this process can lead to constructing game trees that are quite large. However, they do not take a very long time to build and are not beyond analytical comprehension. Because many of the choices that players have in trees are similar at various decision nodes, we can use computer software to simply copy and paste many decision nodes to various points in the tree.[2] Such replication means that there are many different paths to the same outcome, so a lot of terminal nodes will have identical payoffs. While the large game trees may look daunting, we can usually prune the tree substantially and get to something that is a more manageable size. Pruning will be discussed at greater length later, when we discuss how to analyze game trees in Chapter 4 (the Strategy Evaluation stage of the process).

The whole framing process can be completed in one or two days for relatively simple cases, and in a week or two for complex projects. The objective is to have an open, non-black-box process, so regular project team meetings to construct and review game trees as a group are important. Usually having a fairly small project team works best. Three to eight is a good number to target, though ten or twelve may not be unreasonable. Much insight is generated from the structured yet creative conversation entailed in the process, and having this number of perspectives in the discussion should provide sufficiently varied input to understand the issues and generate a creative and expansive frame.

Research and interviews with project team members and other experts typically augment these group discussions. The balance of the time is spent in off-line work to develop and refine game trees to clearly capture the interactions and issues and to facilitate team discussions for better understanding of key issues and insights.

During the framing process, facilitators need to challenge the thinking of team members and push for broad, out-of-the-box thinking. All too often, even diverse teams will

---

(2) I use TreeAge Pro, a decision analysis program, to build trees quickly. I then export trees to PowerPoint and make the adjustments necessary to transform these into game trees.

revert to "business-as-usual" and "don't-rock-the-boat" thinking if not challenged to go further. It is important to create an atmosphere in which everything can be on the table for discussion and team members will be challenged to the point where they sometimes feel uncomfortable. In the end, those who may have experienced discomfort are usually grateful. As one client wrote to me following a lengthy project: "...the last four months have been some of the most eye-opening of my entire career! .... I appreciate your continued efforts to get me to move out of my box and look at the big picture, as confusing and frustrating as that sometimes is."

An added benefit of the process is that it facilitates internal alignment. With Strategic Gaming, project team members speak the same language and use the same logic. Coupled with expansive thinking in an open atmosphere, creative ideas are entertained and taken seriously, and because the logic is transparent, team alignment around new and bold ideas that were not thought possible become feasible. With the logic and value of particular ideas being validated by the process, serious disagreement among team members is rare, even when those ideas may have seemed absurd at the outset. Similarly, those championing particular ideas are usually content to back away when the logic and value are not supported.

While game trees enable the most methodical thinking about action-reaction dynamics, they are sometimes not the best way to facilitate a discussion. Sometimes the issues are so complex or the time available is so limited that it is better to use what are called schematic game trees (see Figure 3.2). Schematic game trees identify players' basic choices, in sequence, as well as chance event uncertainties, but do not map out every possible combination of choices and events. Schematic game trees can be useful to get things started when the issues are quite complex or if there is limited time to interact with a team. Once a schematic game tree is mapped out, game trees can be fleshed out off line and then played back to teams to ensure they accurately capture the dynamics.

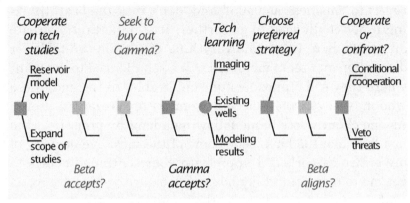

*Figure 3.2: Schematic Game Tree*

To this point, we have discussed the mapping out of choices in a particular sequence. However, sequence may be uncertain. Or, the players could make moves simultaneously, or they could choose sequentially but unbeknownst to one another.

If sequence is uncertain, map out a plausible sequence to get things started. Later in the process, alternative sequences can and should be considered to evaluate the implications, if any, of a different sequence. Sometimes sequence matters, sometimes it does not. This we will see in the next chapter when we discuss the evaluation of game trees.

Simultaneous moves, or choices that are made without another's knowledge (and are thus essentially simultaneous), can be captured with game trees as well, as illustrated in Figure 3.3. There we see that two companies, Alpha and Beta, have to decide whether to launch a product or not, but neither knows the others' decision upon making the choice. To show this simultaneity, the game tree shows Alpha moving "first," which is equivalent to not knowing Beta's choice. In addition, Beta's decision nodes are connected by an "information set" represented by the dashed line, which means that Beta does not know where she is—that is, Beta does not know if Alpha chose to launch. With this setup, we can structure the game to include simultaneous choices; the next chapter will review how to evaluate simultaneous choices in a game tree.

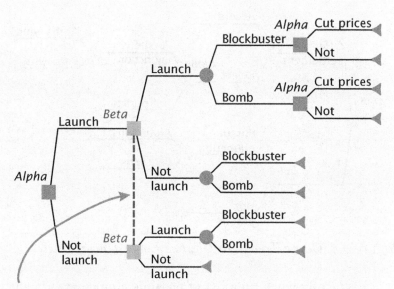

This *"information set"* models Beta's launch decision as one made without knowing whether Alpha decided to launch.

*Figure 3.3: Game Tree with Simultaneous Decisions*

## Uncertainties

Once we have the players' choices mapped out in a reasonable sequence, we refine the game trees, or schematic trees, by incorporating uncertainties. Uncertainties, you will recall, constitute the fourth of the five questions at the heart of Strategic Gaming.

There are two types of uncertainties in a game tree. One type is *chance events*, such as whether a piece of legislation passes, what the price of natural gas will be in the future, or how a judge will rule. The other type of uncertainty has to do with *private information*—what a player knows that another player does not know. The former type of uncertainty is very common in decision analysis and real options. The latter is a unique contribution of game theory and one that is quite important to many strategic situations and negotiations.

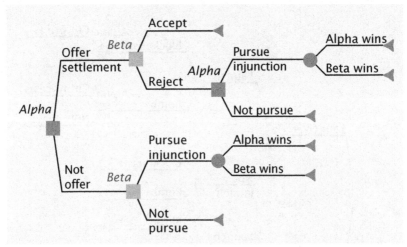

*Figure 3.4: Game Tree with Chance Event Uncertainties*

I typically work up a list of possible chance events with a project team and then determine if they will occur before or after all players have made their moves. If the chance event is revealed after all players have made their moves, it is usually not important to show it in the game tree. Of course, incorporating these uncertainties in an economic model that determines players' payoffs is essential. Whether we show a particular chance event at the end of the tree is a matter of judgment. In a litigation strategy case, I showed the judge's decision (treated as a chance event) at the end of a game tree, shown in Figure 3.4. I did so because how the judge would rule was quite important to the strategy and I wanted to show the client both the potential upside and downside implications of the judge's ruling in favor of Alpha or Beta. The other chance event uncertainties (e.g., market size) were common to all end points, so were not shown in the game tree.

If the outcome of a chance event will occur before a player has made a move, we must show it in the game tree to capture the sequence and see when one or more players have the opportunity to move after learning something. This was shown in Figure 3.3, where Alpha can choose to cut prices upon learning if its product is a blockbuster or bomb.

Figures 3.1 and 3.2 also showed such learning events and how players could exercise what are commonly referred to as options (or real options). Knowing whether a player or players can react to chance events is crucial to mapping out and evaluating the game properly, for options are important and quite common. Oil and gas companies complete seismic studies, which are used as the basis for appraisal drilling and production planning. Pharmaceutical companies, similarly, go through a long, multi-stage process of drug discovery and development. In games, what can be important to consider is whether players can actually exercise options. In some cases, other players will prevent them from doing so.

To fully understand the concept of games with and without chance events, consider the contrast between chess and backgammon. In chess, each player moves, in sequence, and there are no chance events that can intervene. What happens is totally dependent on the players' moves. A game of backgammon, by contrast, involves both player decisions and rolls of the dice. Players thus have to make moves thinking through not only what their opponent may choose to do but also the roll of the dice. Sometimes players will choose to make moves hoping for rolls of the dice that give them the option to make certain subsequent moves. However, in making such a calculation, a player will think about whether his or her opponent will be willing and able to make a move that negates a hoped-for option. Backgammon is thus a game with chance events between each player's moves.

Identifying private information for each of the players is the next step. Private information refers to something one player knows that another does not, and is usually considered to be valuable. Think, for example, of how companies typically require their employees and contractors to sign confidentiality agreements. Private information is important because it means that companies often have to make decisions under uncertainty about competitors' and partners' capabilities and drivers. Private information also means that executives and their companies may signal, or bluff, others, and executives must constantly try to interpret signals from others. By surfacing and analyzing private information issues, Strategic Gaming brings the ubiquitous private information and signaling dimensions of business interactions to the fore, often helping to make sense of other companies' puzzling moves or motivations. At the very least, as we shall see below, evaluation of signaling games helps companies learn from the actions of others, narrowing their uncertainty about others' motivations and likely future choices. This does not mean that Strategic Gaming is a crystal ball, but it can reduce uncertainty substantially and provide insight into how the uncertainty might be further reduced.

An example of private information might be that Alpha knows from internal testing whether a product it is launching is good or has problems, while Beta is uncertain about the quality of Alpha's product and has to decide whether to launch its own product. Or Beta may be uncertain about whether Alpha's value drivers are near-term revenues or long-term NPV. In either case, how players value different possible outcomes is an uncertainty to others.

To illustrate what this means and to show how we would represent private information in a game tree, consider Figure 3.5. Alpha knows its product is great or weak, and it will value the potential outcomes with this knowledge. Hence, we see that Alpha expects, if Beta also launches, to get 600 from launching a great product and 100 from a weak product. The information sets show that Beta is uncertain whether Alpha has a great or weak product, but knows if Alpha has launched. Beta does not know how much it will get from launching if Alpha launches, only that it will receive either −100 or 200, depending on whether Alpha's product is great or weak. If Beta knew that Alpha's product was great, it would not launch, but Beta would prefer to launch if it knew Alpha's product is weak. Beta is therefore torn about what to do because Alpha's information is private. How Beta should evaluate this game and its situation is discussed in the next chapter. For now, what is important is how we can represent private information and signaling with information sets.

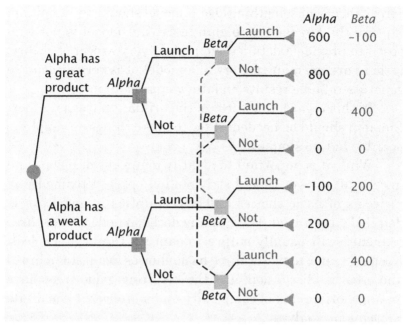

*Figure 3.5: Private Information in a Game Tree*

When we consider private information, it is important that we not only identify our own uncertainties about others, but others' uncertainties about our private information. If we fail to do so, we will have biased the process by treating the issue in a one-sided fashion, not putting ourselves in others' shoes and minds sufficiently.

## Summary and Other Thoughts

The first four questions that Strategic Gaming draws from game theory (players, choices, sequence, and uncertainties), along with the game tree modeling techniques discussed, provide a way to have a structured yet creative conversation among project team members. This facilitates efficient development of a game structure and sets the foundation for alignment.

To get the most out of Dynamic Framing, it is important to strive for broad and expansive thinking while not striving to capture every detail. Whether it is modeling with game trees, spreadsheets, or something else, a model should, by definition, capture the key factors to gain insight. A model is not supposed to provide a detailed picture of every aspect of reality. If there are too many factors in a model, it is very difficult to generate reliable results and draw out useful insights.

In this regard, the words of the brilliant physicist Albert Einstein should be heeded: "I try to make things as simple as possible but no simpler."

While it is important to identify many key decisions and uncertainties over time, I strive to help project teams think in terms of basic choices and uncertainties to avoid overly detailed structuring. Thus, at any decision node, two or three branches will usually suffice to capture the basic choices. Keeping teams to two or three basic choices facilitates a broad and creative discussion, and the resulting game trees have an appropriate mix of complexity and simplicity to facilitate subsequent analysis.

The structure provided by this framing process generally facilitates a creative yet focused discussion among project team members. During the course of the conversation though, it may be tempting to discuss a number of tangentially related issues. How far such conversations should go is a matter of judgment, but it is important to avoid digressing far from the structure and to avoid getting mired in a morass of disconnected thoughts. If we stick to the structure, the process provides an efficient and effective means of gathering the necessary information and generating a solid and creative frame.

As team members work through the framing stage of the process, they:

♦ start to see more clearly how the game would be played out over time,
♦ are able to see things from their competitors' viewpoints, and
♦ can draw out a number of valuable qualitative insights.

The insights may range from "low-hanging fruit" that helps narrow our focus to particular players, choices, and uncertainties (helping us to "prune" the tree), to identifying promising strategic paths that may need further, quantitative investigation.

Project teams are sometimes so delighted with the structure provided and the wealth of qualitative insights gleaned from Dynamic Framing that they want to take action immediately. To do so could be a mistake. In a short period of time and with a modest effort relative to the benefits, many more, and more reliable, insights can be gleaned from completing the Strategic Gaming process. With the quantitative evaluation of games, new insights will not only surface, but may even contravene conclusions reached from the qualitative analysis.

Organizational alignment on a path forward will also be greatly enhanced by thinking through the numbers carefully and by fully understanding the underlying risk factors for each key player. In addition, the numbers play a crucial role in contingency planning, for one has to know when to stop, go, or shift directions in developing a dynamic road map. The numbers help us to know the signposts. Ignoring the numbers can give rise to incomplete, if not sloppy, strategizing that can be dangerous to a company's prospects.

The next chapter thus turns to the second stage in the process, Strategy Evaluation, to see how to undertake the quantitative analysis. That will be followed by a discussion of the third stage in the process, Execution Planning, in which we develop a plan of action that specifies strategies and tactics at every twist and turn in the road, enabling effective shaping and playing of the game of business.

*"...an understanding of 'correct' play may give
us a benchmark for the study of actual behavior."
– Thomas Schelling, 2005 Nobel laureate in Economics,
in his seminal work,* The Strategy of Conflict,
*on the need for strategy informed by game theory.*

4

# Strategy Evaluation

In the second stage of the process, Strategy Evaluation, we seek to make an initial evaluation of our strategic choices, in large part by understanding what the optimal moves of other players should be. This part of the process assumes economic rationality—players choose optimally such that they maximize their expected value. While the assumption is central to game-theoretic analysis, it is only a first step to developing a plan of action. With Strategic Gaming, we typically step outside the game by thinking about how we can change the game and the tactics we can pursue. In so doing we often explore what the implications of relaxing the rationality assumption might be.

Many times though, a game-theoretic analysis insightfully demonstrates that competitors' actions that seem puzzlingly irrational are in fact quite rational. Their behavior was not previously understood because there had not been an adequate appreciation of the competitors' situations, choices, and value drivers. Hence, when we use game theory to understand prospective behavior, it is often the case that our evaluation can be quite predictive. The numbers underpinning the analysis of game trees will often demonstrate that other players have some obvious choices. We can therefore be quite confident about the paths others will choose, given our alternative choices, even if those players are not fully rational.

Of course, in some games the differences in payoffs between others' alternative strategies will be small and our capacity to predict not as strong. Even still, game-theoretic analysis is typically insightful about the tactics that may best elicit information to reduce uncertainty and influence others when we lack predictive clarity. In these cases, the approach provides guidance for developing effective tactics, a task that is central to the final stage of the Strategic Gaming process, Execution Planning, the subject of the next chapter.

For now though, our focus is on the evaluation of games. Evaluation requires that we first address the fifth of five questions drawn from game theory: what are the payoffs to each player for each possible outcome? We populate game trees with these payoffs and quantify uncertainties by assigning probabilities as necessary. We then use game-theoretic techniques to solve and analyze game trees in order to draw out valuable insights. As our games and the underlying numbers are evaluated, they inspire new and deeper conversations among project team members about strategic possibilities and risks and about how to best influence others. This stage in the process provides insight into how others are likely to move and why, helping us to understand the implications of alternative strategic choices in a dynamic, interactive environment.

## Determining Payoffs

To derive payoffs, we use the game trees developed in the Dynamic Framing stage to build economic models similar to those commonly used in the business world. But unlike typical economic models that focus on one company, those used for a Strategic Gaming exercise are done from each player's perspective. So if we would normally do an income statement and use discounted cash flows to determine our net present

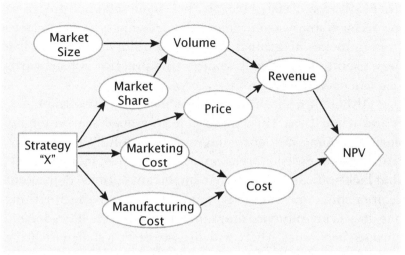

*Figure 4.1: Influence Diagram*

value (NPV), we need to do the same for other players in the game. If others use different value metrics, or we are uncertain what their value metrics are, our economic model should consider alternative value measures for those players. As we shall see, game trees need not use the same value measures for each player. We have the ability to be flexible and should take full advantage of it.

What is the best way to develop an economic model for populating and analyzing game trees? I assume that you are familiar with valuation modeling here, and only discuss the differences versus standard approaches. These differences involve minor adjustments. There are, however, two potential pitfalls with the standard practice of developing economic models for decision analysis.

### Influence Diagrams, Game Trees, and Economic Models

Most practitioners of decision analysis believe that it is useful to sketch an influence diagram—a graphical representation of how decisions and uncertainties determine value (see the example in Figure 4.1).[1] The influence diagram can then be

---

(1) Howard, R. A. and J. E. Matheson, "Influence Diagrams," in R. A. Howard and J. E. Matheson (eds.), *Readings on the Principles and Applications of Decision Analysis*, Volume 2, pages 719-762.

used to draw a decision tree. In fact, some software programs for decision analysis automate the drawing of decision trees from influence diagrams. Though the influence diagram is a very useful tool, I firmly believe this practice is backwards and can even be dangerous.

Although decision analysts sometimes raise their eyebrows when I say this, there is a very good reason for my position. Doing influence diagrams before fully fleshing out game trees or decision trees can easily lead to economic models that lack sufficient attention to important options, dependent relationships, and interactive game dynamics. If the first thing one does is an influence diagram, little will have been done to surface such issues. There will, in essence, be a short-circuiting of the framing and structuring process, whatever that process may be. Almost invariably key issues will be left out.

The second pitfall is that modelers sometimes incorporate many meaningless and often misleading details because they do not have a proper frame. Many modelers assume that it is sufficient to just "throw everything but the kitchen sink" into a model because the power of software and computers enables them to do so. Yet the more complex the model, the more difficult it is to draw out insights. Large, intricate models are also more susceptible to bugs that are difficult to fix or that are never noticed and produce incorrect results. Without a proper frame and structure, influence diagrams and economic models will likely be too simple, too complex, or both.

This is an increasingly common problem for both companies and consulting firms. With the power of computers and a large number of sophisticated programmers who can do lots of detailed and intricate coding, there is an increasing inclination to jump into making assessments and developing economic models without a proper frame and structure. The typical result is deceptively impressive models.

Because framing and structuring shortcuts are taken, if even attempted, options or game issues are seldom uncovered. Thus, complex models consuming thirty megabytes or more of disk space are not uncommon and are at once both too simple and too complex, generating insights that are less than they could be. The recommendations that usually follow from these big models are simple "do this" or "do that" types of statements. While there may be sophisticated analysis to unearth risk factors in the numbers and make a compelling case for particular recommendations, the conclusions cannot provide guidance for wading through a dynamic environment successfully. It is as if the issues are always about what big bet to make. In reality, many issues involve crucial competitor and partner interactions, or the value of options and contingent actions.

One consultant, a highly respected and consummate modeler, told me that it was unnecessary to spend much time learning how to model options because "we don't sell much options work." "Well, of course," I responded, "when you don't look for options they won't be found." I could have said the same thing about interactive game dynamics.

With the Strategic Gaming framing process, we naturally surface the relevant issues and dynamics and develop game trees to structure them. With these game trees, it is straightforward to then sketch out an influence diagram that captures the important dynamics and an appropriate level of complexity, and in turn to construct a useful and insightful economic model.

### Minor Differences in Economic Modeling

As noted, there are some minor differences in constructing Strategic Gaming economic models versus standard modeling.

One involves how to sketch an influence diagram for a game tree. There will be decisions (conventionally represented by squares) for each player in the game, and each of these should be represented. To avoid confusion, it is useful to make clear whose decision is being represented by each square. Meanwhile, private information and chance events are both treated as uncertainties in the influence diagram.

Another obvious difference with standard influence diagrams and economic models is that we must compute values

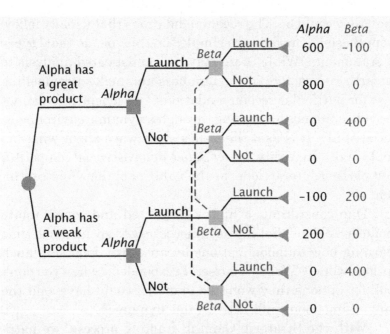

This game tree shows how we model Alpha's private information about whether it has a great or weak product. The dashed lines represent Beta's uncertainty about where she is in the game. In this case, Beta has seen whether Alpha launches or not, but does not know if Alpha has a great or weak product.

*Figure 4.2: Game Tree with Private Information*

for each of the players. This means we have to decide not only what value measure(s) we want to use for ourselves, but what value measure(s) is (are) most likely to be used by other players. We then develop models to capture each player's perspective.

In addition, if there is private information in a game, the player with that private information knows which "type" he or she is, i.e., the outcome of the uncertainty is known to them. Consider the private information game shown in Figure 4.2, in which Alpha may have a great or a weak product. There should be an economic model from Alpha's perspective assuming it has a great product, and another assuming it has a weak product. In other words, Alpha needs to be treated as two different players, even though only one of them is actually playing the game.

| Strategic Gaming Model – Alpha-Beta Game | | | |
|---|---|---|---|

| Game Tree – Decision and Uncertainty Interface | | | |
|---|---|---|---|
| Description | | Value | Option Descriptions |
| **Alpha** | | | |
| Launch / no launch | | 0 | 1 = Yes, 0 = No |
| **Beta** | | | |
| Launch / no launch | | 0 | 1 = Yes, 0 = No |
| | | | |
| **Private Information uncertainties** | | | |
| Product Quality | | 0 | 1 = Great, 0 = Weak |

| Outcome Table | | Payoffs | |
|---|---|---|---|
| Description | | Alpha | Beta |
| **Scenario outcome** | | NPV | NPV |
| Outcome 1 | | 600 | –100 |
| Both launch, great product | | | |
| Outcome 2 | | 800 | 0 |
| A launches, great product | | | |
| Outcome 3 | | 0 | 400 |
| B launches, great product | | | |
| Outcome 4 | | 0 | 0 |
| No launch, great product | | | |
| Outcome 5 | | –100 | 200 |
| Both launch, weak product | | | |
| Outcome 6 | | 200 | 0 |
| A launches, weak product | | | |
| Outcome 7 | | 0 | 400 |
| B launches, weak product | | | |
| Outcome 8 | | 0 | 0 |
| No launch, weak product | | | |

*Figure 4.3: Strategic Gaming Economic Model Interface*

In the economic model, represent all decisions and uncertainties in the game tree (that is, the decision, chance event, and private information nodes) as switches. If each node in a game tree has two choices or potential events, represent each of those possibilities with a 0 or a 1, as is shown in the sample interface in Figure 4.3. Then switch between 0 and 1 to see the effects of different decisions and uncertainties. Since these switches correspond to branches on the game tree, we can populate game trees by going through every possible combination of decisions and uncertainties.[2]

Understanding the outcomes for each player under different scenarios and being able to compare them in game trees can be very insightful in ways this chapter discusses. Game trees are also useful because, in the end, we want a contingency plan, and the trees help us to construct one by understanding how players should move depending on others' choices and the outcome of chance events. Although we will ultimately determine each player's optimal choices, we want to know what to do following learning events and in case another player does not choose optimally.

## Quantifying Uncertainties

We have to assign probabilities for both private information and chance events. Chance event uncertainties shown in the game tree will be treated as switches in the model because they are learning events, and we want to be able to identify what we should do and what others should do after learning something. While probabilities are important for making optimal decisions looking forward, once an event happens we want to know what all players should do from that point forward as well. This is of great importance to developing contingency plans and will give rise to a strategy that is more robust than simply "do this" or "do that."

So, how should we go about assessing and assigning probabilities? For chance events, it is best if we can nail down a particular probability, e.g., there is a 70 percent chance the judge will rule in our favor and a 30 percent chance not. Of course, different members of a project team may well disagree on the proper assessment. In those cases, I elicit opinions from project team members. This enables a sensitivity analysis to see whether and how the different assessments should impact

--------

(2) Unfortunately, there is no publicly available software that can automate the output of payoffs for each of the end nodes in a game tree for each player. With big game trees, I have used simple macros in Excel spreadsheet models to automate the output of payoffs for the many combinations (or, scenarios).

strategy. So we could ask, for example, whether it matters if we believe the judge will rule in our favor with only 50 percent probability rather than 70 percent. It will change our expected value from particular strategies, but may or may not lead us to choose a different strategy. If it does not, then our findings are robust across the different assessments, and the disagreement is not important. If it does matter, then we may try to get additional information to narrow our uncertainty assessments and reach team alignment. How we do so may involve tactical moves that we can craft during the third stage of the process, Execution Planning, which I will talk about in the next chapter.

With uncertainties, we may want to specify a range of possible outcomes.[3] For example, the price of natural gas ten years into the future may be highly uncertain, but we can specify a likely range. One of the most popular and best conventions for determining a range of possible outcomes is to ask what the lowest likely price is—where there is only a 10 percent probability that the price could be lower. We would also ask, similarly, what the highest likely price is—where there is only a 10 percent probability that the price could be higher. Then we want to know a best guess, the median price, which has a 50 percent chance of being higher or lower. These three comprise what is typically referred to as a 10-50-90 range. So, we might say the 10-50-90 for the price of natural gas in five years is $3-$6-$10. We then put the 10-50-90 assessments on to the branches in a tree at an uncertainty node, and assign a probability to each. A standard way of doing so is to assign 25 percent each to the low and high branches, and 50 percent to the median assessment.[4]

Assessments of private information are a little trickier. Private information needs to be defined in terms of how play-

---

(3) See Patrick Leach, *Why Can't You Just Give Me the Number?*, page 27, Discrete versus Continuous Distributions.

(4) See McNamee and Celona, *Decision Analysis for the Professional*, pages 33-36 and Patrick Leach, chapter 4. Some believe that assigning probabilities of 30, 40, and 30 percent is best for the 10-50-90. I don't believe it matters much, particularly for high-level strategy projects.

ers value outcomes. We might say, for example, that there is private information about whether a player is a wimp or a tough guy, and the player's "type" would correspond to different values for outcomes that involve fighting. Wimps would value outcomes with fighting less than tough guys would.

Another example is the one mentioned previously and shown in Figure 4.2. Alpha knows whether it has a good or a weak product, but its competitor Beta does not know which type Alpha is. As can be seen in the game tree, this affects how Alpha values outcomes where its competitor Beta enters the market. If Alpha has a great product and launches, it will make a nice profit (600) if Beta enters, but if Alpha has a weak product and both companies compete in the market, Alpha will lose money (−100). As is usually the case in these games, the quality of Alpha's product also impacts Beta's payoffs. Thus, Beta is uncertain what to do because of the private information. If it launches when Alpha has a great product, Beta will lose money (−100), but it can make 200 if Alpha's product is weak. Beta is therefore torn about whether to enter the market after seeing Alpha's entry because of the private information.

Two types typically make a sufficient distinction for any player with private information. It is usually not useful to make finer distinctions, such as saying that Alpha's product may be good, weak, or somewhere in between. It is technically possible to do so, but can easily make the exercise very complex and it is usually not needed to glean useful and reliable insights.

We should take care to distinguish players' types from the moves they make. It is tempting to equate a player's type with his or her moves, but it is more objective to think in terms of payoffs for different outcomes for each of the types, and then solve the game to see how the types should move given these payoffs. It may well be that a type with a good product should always prefer to launch, as in the example case in Figure 4.2, but there may be circumstances in which a company might not have sufficient incentive to launch even with a good product (e.g., where there is an already saturated, competitive market).

Keeping the payoffs distinct from the decisions in defining types will help us to understand the precise circumstances in which one strategy is better than another.

In eliciting probabilistic assessments for both chance events and private information, it is important to reduce biases that project team members and subject matter experts are likely to have. Often they will provide assessments that are overly optimistic or pessimistic and ranges that are too narrow. This is understandable, for people naturally have a variety of cognitive, psychological, experiential, and organizational biases.

Recognizing these biases is vital to counter them. This may include challenging project team members and subject matter experts by asking hard, skeptical questions about their rationale for a particular assessment. Sometimes it is useful to bring in additional outside expertise to help make the assessments. It is also important to create an atmosphere in which project team members are encouraged to voice their opinions and have them entertained seriously; this will reduce individual and groupthink biases. If the result of this open atmosphere is a lack of alignment on the probabilistic assessments, the sensitivity to probability can be checked. In the end, the results may not be sensitive to the probability, which should foster team alignment on a path forward. If some results are sensitive to different assessments, we will at least get a good sense for where to look further, which will help align the team better than if the views of some team members are down-played or ignored.

Following the advice here should provide reasonable and reliable assessments. In so doing, we will get the most out of our game tree analysis, the subject to which we now turn.

## Analyzing Game Trees

Once we have made the uncertainty assessments and our economic model generates payoffs for the players at each terminal node of a game tree, we can analyze a game tree to see how we and others should move and we can gain insight into the interactive dynamics of the game. Here I use standard techniques from game theory for finding equilibria and analyzing different types of games, but do not rely on a pure game-theory analysis. For reasons and in ways discussed below, Strategic Gaming requires that we go one step beyond academic game theory to understand how players will actually choose in the real world and what we can do to influence others' choices.

Finding equilibria is often a straightforward technical task. However, finding equilibria is a small part of the analysis. There is an art to analyzing games that is far more important, for it can reveal much about the dynamics of the game—why players should be influenced to move one way or another, as opposed to what players should do. Understanding the "why" behind player moves is crucial to having an insightful analysis. In addition, this will usually lead the analyst to think of alternative games that will be useful to analyze. Here too there is an art to creating games that can shed light on certain aspects of a larger problem.

Below I try to avoid being too technical, as I am less concerned with the finer points of game theory than with showing how to quickly and effectively analyze different types of games to draw out practical insights. I thus try to avoid some of the technical verbiage, unless necessary. Game theory texts can provide you with the technical details.[5]

### Game Trees and Backwards Induction

Game theory helps us to look forward and reason back, much as we try to do in playing a game of chess. Many of the game trees we use in Strategic Gaming projects enable us to do this through a process called backwards induction, which shows us the equilibrium strategies for each of the players in a game tree. For those familiar with decision analysis, this is

---

(5) Useful texts include Eric Rasmusen, *Games and Information: An Introduction to Game Theory*, David M. Kreps, *A Course in Microeconomic Theory*, parts III and IV, James D. Morrow, *Game Theory for Political Scientists*, Drew Fudenberg and Jean Tirole, *Game Theory*, Martin J. Osborne and Ariel Rubinstein, *A Course in Game Theory*.

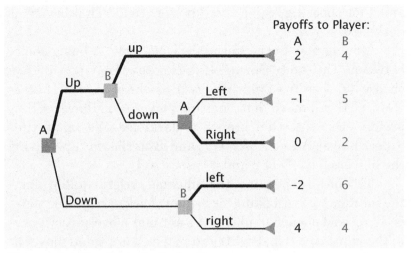

*Figure 4.4: Backwards Induction*

essentially game theory's version of rolling back a tree.

To do backwards induction, we start at the end of our game tree (the right side of the tree, for game and decision trees typically grow sideways, from left to right). At the end of the tree, we ask what the player making the last move should prefer, based on his or her payoffs. We then ask what the player moving prior to that should prefer, given what the player making the last move should choose. We continue with this logic all the way back to the beginning of the tree.

Figure 4.4 illustrates the backwards induction technique. In this, player A has a choice between "Left" and "Right" at the end of the tree. Moving "Left," player A would receive −1, while 0 is the payoff for moving "Right." Thus, A prefers "Right," and the line is darkened to reflect this.

We then move to player B's decision between "up" and "down." B sees that if she chooses "down" she will get a payoff of 2 because her move "down" will be followed by A's move "Right." Moving "up" will get B a payoff of 4. Therefore, B prefers "up" at that decision node, and so we darken that branch.

Where B has a choice between "left" and "right" in the lower node, B would receive a payoff of 6 for choosing "left" and 4 for choosing "right," so B prefers "left." That branch is darkened.

Moving now to the initial decision node, A has a choice between "Up" and "Down." If A chooses "Up," B will then choose "up," so A would receive a payoff of 2. If A chooses "Down," B will move "left," netting player A -2. Player A thus prefers "Up," and that branch is darkened. We would thus expect player A to choose "Up" and B to choose "up," giving the players payoffs of 2 and 4 respectively.

Technically speaking, the subgame perfect equilibrium—the solution we are looking for in doing backwards induction—is comprised of each of player A's optimal moves everywhere in the game tree (Up, Right) and player B's optimal moves at its two decision nodes (up, left). Conventionally, the subgame perfect equilibrium is written (Up, Right; up, left)—Player A's optimal moves (her strategy) are followed after the semi-colon by each of player B's optimal moves at each of its decision nodes. In the equilibrium then, we are specifying each player's strategies, and a strategy specifies a player's moves at each of its decision nodes in the game tree. Strategies are thus not the same as moves unless a player only makes one move in a game.

As some of the moves specified in a strategy may be "off-the-equilibrium path," one might ask, why do we care about moves the players will never make? There are two important reasons.

First, we want to know about moves off-the-equilibrium path to know what our contingency plans should be if other players do not play rationally at particular points in the game. We ultimately want a plan of action that is contingent over time rather than one that simply says "do this" or "do that."

Second, when one analyzes games, it is important to understand the dynamics—why players would be influenced to make particular moves. We thus can see how issues like deterrence, credibility, threats, first-mover advantage, and other factors should influence our and others' decisions. By understanding why, we can find the keen insights that make

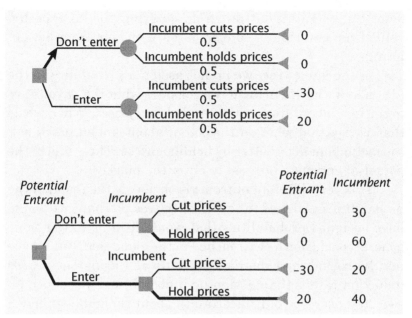

*Figure 4.5: Decision Tree versus Game Tree*

our analysis and subsequent discussions about tactics during execution planning much richer and more realistic.

To more fully appreciate the types of reliable insights we can reach, consider again how game theory compares with decision analysis. In prior chapters I talked about how game theory better models interactive decisions between two or more players. Treating other players' decisions as choices rather than uncertainties has both technical and practical benefits. Without having to assign numerous probabilities to solve the game, we can identify quite a few choices for each player over time. Moreover, without having to assign probabilities to other players' moves, we take a great deal of the subjectivity that can lead us astray out of the process while employing a more sensible, chess-like logic to our analysis.

These points are illustrated by the simple example in Figure 4.5. There we see that a potential entrant is choosing whether to enter a market dominated by an incumbent who may choose to cut prices. In the decision tree, we can see that the 0.5 probability that the incumbent will cut prices should deter the potential entrant from entering, for its expected value from entering is –5 (compared with zero from not entering).

In the game tree, we do not assign a probability to the incumbent's move. Instead, we consider what the payoffs are to the incumbent from cutting or holding prices. When we do that, we see that whether the potential entrant enters or not, the incumbent does better by holding prices. Thus, it is in the potential entrant's interest to enter the market.

This very different outcome is obviously the result of the probabilities assigned in the decision tree. Perhaps we would have assigned probabilities that would lead us to the same general conclusion as we reached in the game tree. But maybe not. By considering the likely payoffs and using backwards induction rather than assigning probabilities, we reduce biases and decrease our uncertainty about the implications of a strategic move.

Let's now look at two other examples of games in which we can use backwards induction to determine equilibria and drive analysis. I show them here to make a simple but very important point: the equilibrium is not everything. It is important to analyze the dynamics of the game and consider what the results tell us, and then check to verify that the results are sensible.

Consider first the game in Figure 4.6, known as the Centipede Game. Players A and B have to decide whether to continue or stop at each decision node. If one does backwards induction, it is clear that both players would choose to stop at every decision node (and those branches are darkened). The game would never get going since player A would stop on the first move of the game, thereby ending the game with both players receiving 3. Yet both players could do better if the game continued to the end. We can see that the reason for this suboptimal outcome is that each player has an incentive to stop the game at each decision node, and that continuing the game when the other has the same incentive is costly to both players.

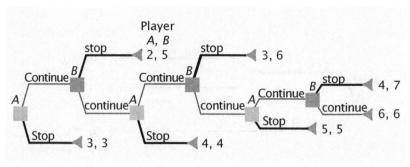

*Figure 4.6: Centipede Game*

If all we did was determine the equilibrium and then make a prescription for player A from that, we would simply tell the player to stop immediately. But to do so would be insufficient. A game tree, like any model, is a simplification of reality. As such, it excludes many possibilities, and some of these could not easily have been recognized without the simple game tree as a heuristic. And so by understanding why we are getting this suboptimal result, we can find ways we might change the game.

In the Centipede game we might ask: is there a way for A to communicate with B and forge a legally binding agreement to continue the game for a certain period of time so that there would be a larger win-win? Or, could they each make a public commitment that would have significant reputational consequences to a player that backs down from the commitment? These sorts of questions, and others, could change the game in a mutually beneficial way. Simply knowing the equilibrium is not enough for getting the most out of our game trees.

Another important game is the Chain Store Paradox shown in Figure 4.7. This contribution by Reinhard Selten, who shared the Nobel Prize with John Nash in 1994, is a game that shows a chain store incumbent should not fight a potential entrant. While the incumbent's payoff is half of what it would be if the entrant stayed out (50 rather than 100), acquiescing is better than the costs of fighting. Selten saw this result as paradoxical, and for good reason. If the chain store didn't fight an entrant, then there might be other entrants, and soon

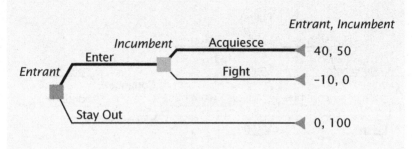

*Figure 4.7: Chain Store Paradox*

its market share would dwindle substantially. The game as set up only shows one round with one possible entrant, yet the situation is surely a multiple round game with multiple potential entrants. The counterintuitive result thus seems to be misleading.

This misleading counterintuitive result provides an important lesson: one should be able to explain and justify counterintuitive insights we derive from game tree models. If we have questions about our results, as we do with Selten's game, we must ask what key factors, if any, the game tree and economic model that produces the payoffs leave out or misrepresent. Are the numbers based on a single year's profits or profits over a long period of time (e.g., NPV for 15 years of cash flows)? Are there other potential entrants? If the numbers are long-term and there is only one potential entrant over that period of time, it may well make sense for the chain store to acquiesce rather than fight. But if there are other potential entrants, we would want to show their options in the game tree as well and understand all the players' payoffs for the refined game and over a sufficient period of time.

The general point, then, is to question results and to avoid being satisfied too easily. A critical eye will help to reveal whether there are gaps in the analysis that are caus-ing misleading conclusions. It is then possible to refine game trees and economic models. Or it should at least be possible to have a sensible conversation about the limits of the analy-sis. With some projects I have worked, it became clear that the games I was analyzing with client teams were one part of a much larger picture. We could not model everything and refined game trees were not necessary or appropriate. Yet it was sufficient to understand that the games we were analyzing comprised one part of a much broader game. Though we were able to highlight the trade-offs and implications in only one part of the larger game being played by the company, the quantification and deep analysis were a tremendous help for decision makers, who could see how the implications of the game at hand fit with big picture issues and priorities.

These kinds of issues have been quite common in project work in which I have been engaged. To provide just one example, an oil and gas company I worked with was considering divestment of some of its equity in an asset and was considering different potential partners. A deal with one prospective partner was seen to be slightly profitable, while we expected a slight loss in a prospective deal with another. However, management felt that the latter deal might make more sense given that it could help with the broader global goals it had to cultivate partnerships with that company. The trade-offs were transparent and could help decision makers weigh them against other corporate priorities and goals.

### Backwards Induction with Chance Events

We can also use backwards induction when we have chance events in our game tree. The process is similar, but we have to calculate expected values (EVs) looking forward when chance events are involved. For those uninitiated with expected values, they are simply the probability weighted value of different possible outcomes. Thus, if we are entered in a lottery in which we have a 0.25 probability of winning $100 and 0.75 probability of winning nothing, our EV is (0.25 x $100) + (0.75 x $0) = $25. We will never actually receive $25; it is simply our expected value.

To solve a game with chance events using backwards induction, consider Figure 4.8. Beta's decision to increase drilling or not at the top node is determined by the EV look-

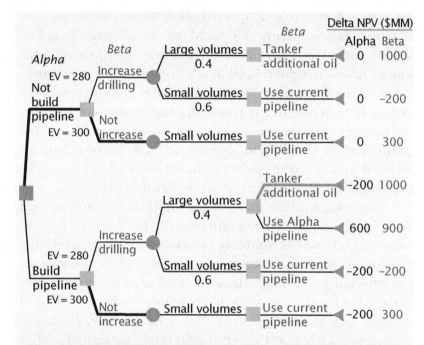

This game tree shows that Alpha can build a pipeline, creating a potentially valuable option for "exporting" large volumes of oil and gas. But, whether this option will be beneficial also depends on whether Beta decides to increase drilling; in this case, we would not expect Beta to do so.

*Figure 4.8: Backwards Induction with Chance Events*

ing forward. Beta will get 300 for sure if she does not increase drilling. She will get 1000 with 0.4 probability and -200 with 0.6 probability if she increases drilling, an expected value of 280. Hence, since the 300 from not drilling is higher than the expected value of 280, that is the optimal choice at that node.

At Beta's lower node the result is the same, but there's a twist. As we look forward, we also have to see whether Beta should choose to tanker additional oil or, if increased drilling leads to large volumes, use the Alpha pipeline. Beta prefers to tanker the oil, so the expected value calculations are identical. We then work back to Alpha's initial decision in the game, and we see that the choice is between receiving zero from not building the pipeline and losing 200 since Beta would not use the new Alpha pipeline. Alpha should choose not to build.

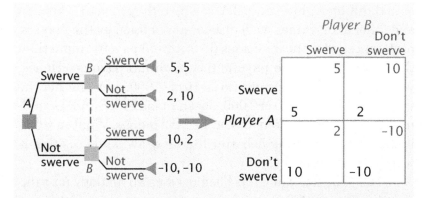

*The dashed line, an information set, indicates that B does not know what option A has chosen, or that the two players are moving simultaneously.*

*Figure 4.9: Simultaneous Moves in Extensive and Normal Form*

### Simultaneous Play Games and Nash Equilibria

In some cases, players make simultaneous moves or their decisions are essentially equivalent to simultaneous moves. For instance, in a sealed bid auction, each player is making a simultaneous move because the players do not know what is in others' envelopes. Or, two companies may decide secretly on innovation investments to their respective product lines, but not know one another's decision until each launches the improved products.

We cannot use backwards induction to solve a simultaneous play game. Instead, we use what is called the normal, or strategic, form (a matrix) to solve the game. As shown in Figure 4.9, if we had a tree in which two players are shown to be moving simultaneously (as the information set depicts), we would put their strategies on two sides of a matrix. Where the strategies intersect are the potential outcomes. So if each player has two strategies, there will be four outcomes, a 2 x 2 matrix, as in Figure 4.9.

The payoff structure here comprises that of the famous game of Chicken (discussed in Chapter 2). In the cells of the matrix are numbers, which represent the payoffs to each player for each of the four possible outcomes in the game. What is important about these numbers is not the size of the actual numbers, but the order in which they appear. Chicken and other 2 x 2 games we'll discuss are defined by the players' preferences over the outcomes (i.e., ordinal payoffs) more than the actual size of the payoffs (i.e., cardinal payoffs). Hence, whether the crashing scenario is -10 or -1000, and whether the value of winning is 10 or 1000, doesn't matter for understanding the game of Chicken and other 2 x 2 games. What matters is the order—winning is better than a draw, and crashing is worse than losing the game.[6]

The Chicken game has been used as an analogy for talking about such things as crises in international affairs and labor-management negotiations. For example, in the Cuban Missile Crisis, Soviet leader Nikita Khrushchev presumably "swerved" in the face of John Kennedy's perceived resolve. JFK's appearance on television to demand the withdrawal of the missiles certainly enhanced this perception. By going on television and putting his personal reputation on the line, Kennedy was, in effect, throwing the steering wheel out the window to show Khrushchev he was not going to "swerve." Seeing that, Khrushchev backed down. (Truthfully, the reality was a bit more complicated than that.) With labor-management negotiations and strikes, there are similar resolve issues and a question of which party will blink first.

To solve Chicken and other simultaneous play games, we look for Nash equilibria. A Nash equilibrium is an outcome in which no player has an incentive to deviate (choose a different strategy) given the strategy of the other players. Put a different way, it is an outcome that is a best response for every player in the game given the strategy of each of the other players. (This concept is the contribution that won John Nash the Nobel Prize; the subgame perfect equilibria we looked for using backwards induction are a subset, or refinement, of the Nash equilibrium solution.)

---

(6) When we talk about mixed strategies, games with incomplete information, and repeated games, we will see that the size of the payoffs can matter. But for basic Nash equilibrium analysis (in pure strategies) of 2 x 2 games, ordinal payoffs are what matter.

We can go through each of the four boxes in the Chicken game of Figure 4.9 to see which is a Nash equilibrium. The bottom right cell (the outcome in which neither player swerves), is obviously not in equilibrium since it is the worst outcome for both players. Both players have an incentive to swerve given that the other is not swerving. In the top left cell, both players swerve and there is a draw. This is not in equilibrium either, for both players have an incentive to not swerve given that the other has swerved. The bottom left and top right cells are both equilibria. If player A does not swerve, player B would want to swerve to avoid the worst outcome. Similarly, player A would prefer to swerve if player B does not. These two outcomes are thus best responses for both players and so are Nash equilibria.

One might be confused with these results. How can there be two equilibria? What does that tell us? Why is this a reasonable solution given that it is not giving us a prediction for how the players should play the game? In fact, it seems intuitively plausible that any of the four outcomes might actually be the result rather than one of the two equilibria.

These are all fair points. What should be recognized is that a Nash equilibrium is not necessarily a prediction for how the players should play the game, only whether a strategy is a best response to other players' strategies. Understanding a game's dynamics—why we get these equilibria—is where the real insight comes from. And that is what is valuable about Nash equilibria. To reiterate a point I made earlier, finding equilibria is only a small first step. It is far more important to understand why we see particular equilibria and what those tell us about how players should play the game.

So let us think about what is going on in the game of Chicken, which provides significant insights despite (and in some respects because of) its simplicity and multiple equilibria. One thing the game of Chicken shows us is that it is important to be a first mover (if possible). Or, if one cannot unconditionally commit to the first move, it is crucial to demonstrate resolve to "not swerve." If we were to use Strategic

Gaming in a project and find something similar to a game of Chicken, we could talk in depth about ways we might try to throw the steering wheel out the window to show resolve. Indeed, in one project for a power company we explored a complex set of interactions and realized that the key issue in a complex game boiled down to something similar to a game of Chicken. As we came to understand this, we had extensive and rich discussions with the client team about whether the company should start construction of a project, at substantial cost, to demonstrate resolve, or whether public statements to initiate construction might be sufficient to deter others. The analysis led the company to entertain more proactive and bolder initiatives than it would have otherwise.

The most famous 2 x 2 game is the Prisoner's Dilemma, discussed in Chapter 2 and shown again in Figure 4.10. As you may recall, in the Prisoner's Dilemma, two criminals are captured, and each is placed in separate rooms and asked to turn states' evidence on one another. If neither finks on the other, the District Attorney will only be able to put each away for one year on minor charges. So the District Attorney makes an offer to each. If either finks on his accomplice, he'll go free while the other will be put away for 10 years. If both fink on each other, they will each get 7-year sentences.

Let us solve for the Nash equilibrium in this game using the approach discussed above. We see that in the top left cell, the prisoners would each get just 1 year in jail if they "cooperate" by choosing not to fink on one another. This is not a Nash equilibrium, for each has an incentive to fink on the other when the other does not fink. The bottom left and top right cells are not in equilibrium, for neither player wants to avoid finking and receive what is commonly referred to as the "sucker's payoff"—the long jail sentence of 10 years—when the other player finks, and so there is an incentive to fink. That leaves us with the bottom right cell, which is a Nash equilibrium—both fink on each other. Neither player has an incentive to not fink when the other finks, for they would be stuck with the sucker's payoff. Yet this outcome is suboptimal for the prisoners, for if they both could trust one another to

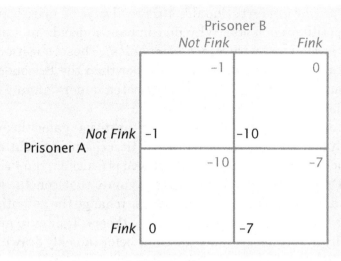

*Figure 4.10: Prisoner's Dilemma*

"cooperate" by not finking, then they would get off with much lighter sentences. That is their dilemma.

The Prisoner's Dilemma is seen to have broad applicability. In business, some would say the Prisoner's Dilemma can explain price wars or why two companies might fail to forge a strategic alliance. It has been used to explain why, in international arms control negotiations, the central issue is one of verification, for countries do not want to disarm unilaterally and lose an arms race.

To be sure, the appeal of the Prisoner's Dilemma is warranted. It can help explain why two players may find it difficult to cooperate and, perhaps more importantly, it can generate valuable conversations about ways to formalize, or build, trust. As was the case with the Chicken game, the value of the Nash equilibrium is more in the insights it helps us generate about players' incentives and how they might seek to change the game.

There are limits to the Prisoner's Dilemma that should be recognized and understood as well. In particular, it is often an oversimplification of reality that may be misleading. For example, the Prisoner's Dilemma might be an adequate description of a price war at a given point in time, but why did the price war start? Shouldn't there always be price wars in competitive markets? Why do companies decide to start or end price wars with other companies? These questions suggest that the issues are much deeper than the Prisoner's Dilemma and require a more sophisticated understanding of the situation to find a solution.

I would thus caution those attempting to use game theory that, while it may be tempting to look at a complex situation and conclude that the game being played is Chicken, the Prisoner's Dilemma, or some other 2 x 2 game, that conclusion may be dangerously misleading and shortchange the potential insights that can be gleaned from game theory. It pays to methodically frame and evaluate the game before quickly drawing on simple analogies. A more rigorous approach to structuring the game often leads to much different and richer results.[7]

### Games with Private Information

Many times we will not know important factors that others know, or perhaps we may have such "private information." Situations with private information are quite common. For instance, in negotiations we typically do not know the lowest price our negotiating partner would be willing to sell to us. Likewise, the partner would be uncertain of the highest price we'd be willing to pay. Or, we may not know whether or when a competitor may launch a new technology. Or perhaps we are an oil and gas explorer that has acquired proprietary seismic data for an oil field prospect. In all these cases, one or more players in a game are uncertain about how others value particular outcomes because there is private information.

An important subset of all games with private information is signaling games. In signaling games, players have

(7) Note that normal form games with more than two players and/or when players have more than the two strategies found in 2 x 2 games are possible, and though they are bigger and take more time to solve and analyze, they may well be necessary and appropriate. The Nash equilibrium is found with the same technique described above, in which we consider whether each player's strategy for a given cell is a best response given the other players' strategies.

an opportunity to signal something about how they value outcomes. They may also be able to bluff. In business, and everyday life, we often talk about what others may be signaling, or if they are bluffing, and about what sorts of signals we should send. Such assessments are crucial, but they are difficult to make.

So how should we decide, given our or others' private information? How can we evaluate possible signals? What sorts of signals should we send? Analyzing signaling games can provide a methodical, sensible, and insightful way of looking at these situations and addressing such questions.

Consider again the signaling game in Figure 4.2, reproduced below in slightly altered form as Figure 4.11. In this game, Alpha knows whether it has a great or weak product in its pipeline, and needs to decide whether to launch. Beta does not know the quality of Alpha's product and needs to decide whether to launch its similar, but somewhat weak, product. If Alpha's product is great, and Beta launches, Beta would lose a substantial amount of money while Alpha would do well. If Alpha's product is weak and both launched, Beta would do well and Alpha would lose money. Both players would do well if they were the only ones to launch.

To fully and properly solve this and similar games requires a fairly complex Bayesian updating process, which was a contribution of John Harsanyi, who received the Nobel Prize with Nash and Selten in 1994. I will not go through the complete academic solution to this type of game here. (In fact, game theory texts do not even show explicitly how to solve these games in a methodical fashion.) Though I have developed a straightforward algorithm for solving these games, and have taught it to advanced game theory students and incorporated it into a computer program I designed called "Game Solver," the algebraic calculations and software are typically not essential. I have found that there are shortcuts that can usually help us draw out the necessary intuitions without undertaking the extensive calculations required to solve such games. Hence, the focus here is on the shortcuts that will typically yield useful insights in a Strategic Gaming exercise.

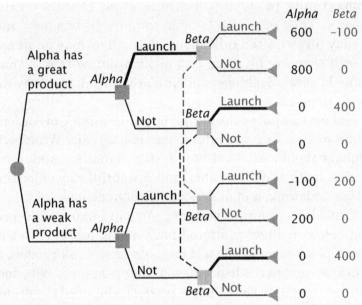

Beta's decision to launch is easy if Alpha does not launch, but Beta is uncertain whether to launch if Alpha does.

For Alpha, the decision to launch is easy if it has a great product, but if its product is weak, the success or failure of its launch decision is contingent on what Beta does. So, Alpha might be able to successfully "bluff."

*Figure 4.11: Signaling Game*

What we do is look at "what if" scenarios assuming complete information (i.e., no private information). That is, we ask what the players would do if they were certain what "world" they were in, with the worlds being defined by the possible types of player we are uncertain about. In some cases, we might realize that all types of players should do the same thing regardless of the uncertainty. In other cases, behavior could be perfectly reflective of a player's type (i.e., a clear signal). In still other cases, it may depend on the situation, but at least we can understand the value of information, and this can help us in developing strategies and tactics.

To illustrate, consider the game in Figure 4.11. In this we would ask, what would happen if Beta knew Alpha had a great product? Then, what if Beta knew that Alpha had a weak product?

If Alpha had a great product, Alpha would clearly prefer to launch, regardless of Beta's move, since Alpha would make 600 or 800, depending on whether Beta launched or not. Thus, the branch is darkened to denote Alpha's dominant strategy of launching if it has a great product. Beta would not want to launch if it knew Alpha's product was great as Beta would receive -100 rather than 0 for not launching, but would want to launch if Alpha's product was weak as Beta would then get 200. Note that Alpha does better (800 vs. 600) if Beta does not launch, so if Alpha has the great product, it should want to do everything it can to convince Beta of this. Perhaps Alpha would share product test data with Beta and make early public statements committing to launch its product to deter Beta.

Meanwhile, if Beta knew Alpha's product was weak, it would want to launch no matter what Alpha does, though it would prefer that Alpha not launch (400 vs. 200). So, what this suggests is that Beta should seek Alpha's product test data, and this request could be rationalized to Alpha as a win-win since Beta would be deterred from entering the market if the product was great. With a weak product, Alpha might want to "bluff" in this scenario, and so might wish to make a public statement of its intention to launch, putting its credibility on the line if it were to not launch. Just like placing a high bet in poker when one doesn't have a good hand, this bluff might deter Beta.

As the discussion above suggests, the game provides tactical insights for both players about whether and how to reveal or elicit "private information." Indeed, one somewhat counterintuitive finding in these games is that it may be beneficial for a player like Alpha to avoid secrecy about its intentions and capabilities, and that secrecy may actually be a signal of weakness. Similarly, Beta should seek to elicit information from Alpha and test Alpha's reactions in order to make a decision about launching.

Though such tactics are often quite effective, we will not in all cases be able to tactically "change the game" to sufficiently influence perceptions or reduce uncertainties. We would in those cases have to make a judgment about what our best move is, and here is where the "proper" Bayesian game-theoretic solution and Game Solver could be useful. That said, I have seldom found it necessary to go to that level in a client engagement. Following the suggestions above, and thinking about the tactics that such a game gives rise to, usually provide the structure and insights necessary for having rich conversations that enable the development of a proactive and robust action plan.

### What About Mixed Strategies?

To this point, we have only discussed strategic moves in terms of "pure strategies," as opposed to "mixed strategies." With pure strategies, a player has a distinct move or set of moves she should pursue. With a mixed strategy, a player will choose one way some of the time, and another way part of the time. In a sense, the player flips a coin, although the coin may or may not be fair-sided (for example, it could be that a player should choose one strategy 10 percent of the time and another 90 percent of the time).

When and why are mixed strategies important? Only rarely do we find mixed strategies of relevance in Strategic Gaming engagements. Much of the reason is that most Strategic Gaming analysis requires only fairly straightforward backwards induction, which gives us pure strategies. Moreover, we are not typically looking at situations in which companies are going to be making similar decisions many times, thus having an opportunity and the desire, potentially, to play a mixed strategy.

That is not to say mixed strategies do not exist in the real world. When you call a company's customer support line, for instance, there is often a recording that says the call may be monitored to ensure adequate customer service. Companies do not monitor every call, for that would be prohibitively costly. But by randomly monitoring a portion of the calls, agents are likely to be courteous and helpful on a regular basis. Similarly, police do not try to catch speeders in a certain location and at a certain time every day. They sometimes set the speed trap, and sometimes not. If they were always in a particular location at a given time, all drivers would come to know that, and the police would never nab anyone. The police thus have an incentive to pursue a mixed strategy.[8]

While mixed strategies are employed in the real world, we seldom encounter such situations in Strategic Gaming engagements. But if in conducting a Strategic Gaming exercise it becomes apparent that a company has a choice of this flavor—one in which it is making a particular choice more than once and doing the same thing repeatedly could be counterproductive—we would then want to determine the optimal mixed strategy. Though we seldom encounter these situations, let's review the game-theoretic solution technique in the interest of completeness.[9]

Consider the game in Figure 4.12, where player A can be nasty or nice, and player B can monitor A's behavior or not. If you look for Nash equilibria in pure strategies, you will not find one. In every cell there is an incentive for one of the players to deviate. It is thus necessary to look for the Nash equilibrium in mixed strategies. The solution is found by finding an optimal mix for each player that makes the other player indifferent between her alternative strategies. Thus we do the following for the game:

---

(8) There is another side to these stories as well. It may be that customer support agents and drivers also have an incentive to play a mixed strategy. An agent who doesn't value his or her job highly and encounters an obstreperous customer may "lose it" and risk the boss's anger by being rude to the customer. Or, a driver who is late for an important meeting at work may find it worth the risk of speeding and getting a ticket. For a discussion of these issues and an interesting comparison of how decision theory and game theory come to much different conclusions, see George Tsebelis, "The Abuse of Probability in Political Analysis: The Robinson Crusoe Fallacy," *American Political Science Review* 83, 1 (March, 1989): pages 77-91.

(9) Technically speaking, games may have both pure and mixed strategy equilibria. For example, the game of Chicken has two pure strategy equilibria, and one mixed. However, I subscribe to the belief that many share, that where there are pure strategy equilibria, they are more sensible. Generally speaking, we should be concerned about mixed strategy equilibria when we find games that do not have a pure strategy equilibrium.

|  | Player B | |
|  | *Monitor* | *Not Monitor* |
|---|---|---|
| | 50 | 150 |
| Nice | 50 | 50 |
| | 100 | -100 |
| Nasty | -50 | 100 |

Player A is labeled on the left with rows *Nice* and *Nasty*.

*Figure 4.12: Game with No Nash Equilibria in Pure Strategies*

♦ Set the probability that player A chooses Nice to $x$, and Nasty to $1 - x$; for B, Monitor is probability $y$ and Not Monitor is $1 - y$. Note that $x$ and $y$ are each between 0 and 1.

♦ Player A then has the following EV equations:

  – $EV_{Nice} = 50\,y + 50\,(1 - y)$ (Note: the first 50 is the payoff to player A for being nice when B chooses Monitor, which it will do so with probability $y$; the other 50 is the payoff to player A for being nice when B chooses not to monitor, which it will do so with probability $1 - y$.)

  – $EV_{Nasty} = -50\,y + 100\,(1 - y)$

  – Setting equal to find where Player A is indifferent between Nice and Nasty, and solve for $y^*$, the optimal amount B should monitor. This gives us $y^* = 1/3$.

♦ Player B has the following EV equations:

  – $EV_{Monitor} = 50\,x + 100\,(1 - x)$

  – $EV_{Not\ Monitor} = 150\,x + (-100)\,(1 - x)$

  – Setting these equations equal to find where Player B is indifferent between Monitor and Not Monitor gives us the optimal amount A should be Nice, $x^* = 2/3$.

In sum, the results say that player B should monitor one-third of the time, and player A should be nice two-thirds of the time. What you may also notice from these results is that the size of the payoffs, contrary to what we saw in determining pure strategy equilibria in simultaneous games, will matter in determining mixed-strategy equilibria. Indeed, the size of the payoffs and the solution can lead us to somewhat counter-intuitive results and useful prescriptions. In this game, we can see that if the penalty to player A for being nasty and getting caught by a monitoring player B is more severe, let's assume –150 instead of –50, the amount player B will monitor decreases from a third to a fifth. Hence, if player B can make the punishment to A for getting caught higher, monitoring will be less essential.

### *What About Repeated Games?*

Companies are often engaged in ongoing strategic inter-action. As such, many suggest it is inappropriate to model interactions as if the companies are playing a game only once. There is some merit to this point, and there is a large amount of literature on the subject of repeated games. In fact, Thomas Schelling shared his 2005 Nobel with Robert Aumann, who was noted for his insightful contributions in the area of repeated games.

One of the most interesting studies on repeated games was done by Robert Axelrod, who held a computer tournament to determine the optimal strategy in a repeated (or, iterated) Prisoner's Dilemma, in which players could choose to cooperate or to defect.[10] As mutual defection is the equilibrium outcome of a one-shot Prisoner's Dilemma, Axelrod wanted to see if cooperation could emerge in a repeated Prisoner's Dilemma. What he found was that one of the simplest of the strategies submitted in the tournament, Tit-for-Tat, was the best. In Tit-for-Tat, a player cooperates in round one, and then does whatever her counterpart did in the previous round. If the other cooperated, the Tit-for-Tat strategy calls for continued

---

(10) Robert Axelrod, *The Evolution of Cooperation.*

cooperation. If the other chose to defect, defection in round two would be the choice under the Tit-for-Tat strategy decision rule. This strategy of reciprocity, or conditional cooperation, would continue as long as the game was repeated.

Axelrod demonstrated that Tit-for-Tat could give rise to cooperation in a repeated Prisoner's Dilemma if two players "have a sufficiently large chance to meet again so that they have a stake in their future interaction." Not only would Tit-for-Tat strategies be an equilibrium pair if the shadow of the future were sufficiently long, but each player could do better than if they pursued the dominant strategy of defection in a one-shot Prisoner's Dilemma. In fact, Tit-for-Tat proved better when paired against all other entries in the tournament. Axelrod concluded that its robustness stemmed from "its combination of being nice, retaliatory, forgiving, and clear." Axelrod explained, "Its niceness prevents it from getting into unnecessary trouble. Its retaliation discourages the other side from persisting whenever defection is tried. Its forgiveness helps restore mutual cooperation. And its clarity makes it intelligible to the other player, thereby eliciting long-term cooperation."[11]

These findings are very powerful and intuitively appealing. They make sense and, in many respects, seem to be right for many interactions in which we as individuals and companies engage. But where and how are repeated games useful? How do they fit into a Strategic Gaming exercise? In short, I don't believe a formal treatment of repeated games in Strategic Gaming engagements is useful, but my clients and I pay heed to repeated interactions and the lessons of work by Axelrod and others.

It is clearly the case that many companies are repeatedly interacting with one another, and the fact that there may be an ongoing relationship should enter our analysis. So, for example, just because one course of action appears in our games to be the best for maximizing value in a given situation, we may not want to pursue it if we think it can spoil relations

---

(11) Axelrod, *The Evolution of Cooperation*, page 54.

with a company we interact with regularly. Or, perhaps it is important to take a strong stand that costs us some value in the near term vis-à-vis a partner because it can help us set a precedent and establish credibility in future interactions. We will want to have such conversations, drawing on the lessons of repeated games.

I regularly have such conversations with my clients, but do not engage in a formal treatment of repeated games. The reason is that companies may repeatedly interact, but the choices they have will vary over time and under different circumstances. Repeated games repeat the same game over and over. Instead, I find it prudent to sketch a game that has two or three stages. I believe it is usually more realistic to think of games as having multiple stages in which the choices in the initial stage are different than in subsequent stages, and the payoffs are affected by choices made in each stage. Such multi-stage games are more realistic and insightful than repeated games are in most situations I have encountered. And in this way, I avoid repeating the same game over and over (as Axelrod does), but also avoid falling into the trap of the Chain Store Paradox.

The results of work in the area of repeated games are therefore a useful reminder as we model and develop strategies and tactics. However, I find repeated games are not essential or appropriate to model in a Strategic Gaming exercise. While companies may repeatedly interact, the choices they have will vary over time and come under different circumstances. By contrast, work in the area of repeated games repeats the same game, which is not appropriate for understanding most situations. In addition, the situations encountered typically have a much more complex set of decisions than a Prisoner's Dilemma or other simple game that can feasibly be repeated. In fact, even if one can repeat a complex game, those tend to have so many equilibria that it is often impossible to draw out useful insights.

We certainly must recognize when interactions between players are ongoing, but this does not mean they are repeatedly making the same choices. Hence, from a modeling standpoint, repeated games are not useful for most situations in which Strategic Gaming should be applied. However, the lessons from the literature on repeated games and from the Chain Store Paradox must be kept in mind to have a sufficiently broad, long-term perspective.

## Exploit Game Theory's "Rigorous Flexibility"

One implication of the discussion in this chapter is that there are a variety of game structures one can employ in an analysis to help capture the essence of the situation at hand. And in most cases, no single game tree or other game model will adequately capture the situation or enable us to analyze a situation thoroughly. I will typically consider a series of game models that look at a situation from a variety of angles, using different assumptions, to have a clear understanding of the situation and of the robustness of results.

In doing such analyses, I am taking advantage of what Professor Robert Pahre and I once referred to as game theory's "rigorous flexibility." Game theory's central concepts and mathematical logic provide the rigor, but there is substantial flexibility in applying the method to specific problems. Game theory does not require any particular assumptions about who the important players are or what interests players have; the most salient features of the substantive problem being examined can drive our analysis. Game theory's rigorous flexibility lets us be flexible in our modeling choices while we exploit the theoretical rigor of the method.

When we construct and analyze a series of game models, game theory's rigor makes it relatively easy to compare the models to draw out implications that go beyond those found in individual models. It enables us to see whether results are robust or contingent, and if the latter, contingent upon what. If a group of models yields similar results despite making very different assumptions, we can have substantial confidence in the robustness of the results. If a group of game models has different assumptions and produces different results, then the models are suggestive of the conditions under which particular results hold, guiding us to make further inquiries or to refine our assessments of critical factors.[12]

For the analyst employing Strategic Gaming, this means that it is often very useful to develop a game model that focuses on general aspects of the larger situation and then construct a series of models that capture the situation from different angles, making a variety of assumptions. The set of game models will produce more reliable insights than will a large game that tries to capture everything.

## Beyond the Game Models: Drilling Down on the Numbers

Just as we should look at a variety of game trees or matrices, we should also look at the payoffs to our game models from a variety of angles to glean further insight. It is important to drill down into the numbers to identify risk factors and to better understand where value is being gained or lost (for both ourselves and other players). Those with strong decision analysis and/or economic modeling backgrounds will be familiar with such techniques. I will only briefly discuss how to work with the numbers in a Strategic Gaming analysis. More detailed discussion can be found in references on decision analysis.[13]

Typically initial game analysis uses payoffs that are deterministic numbers. What this means is that we assume the P50 (base case or median value) outcome for chance event uncertainties. While we should have included 10-50-90 assessments of uncertainty inputs in our economic model, we will typically look first at payoffs for the players as if the P50 actually happened. (A key exception to this, however, is if a chance event happens before all players' moves have been made, i.e., a learning event. In that case, we will consider

---

(12) See Robert Pahre and Paul A. Papayoanou, "Using Game Theory to Link Domestic and International Politics," *Journal of Conflict Resolution* 41, 1 (February 1997), pages 4-11.

(13) See, for example, McNamee and Celona, *Decision Analysis for the Professional*, especially chapter 6, and Patrick Leach, *Why Can't You Just Give Me the Number?*

what should happen depending on what is learned, and what players should do from an expected value standpoint prior to the learning event.)

Deterministic analysis is a very useful first step. It can help us understand the magnitude of differences between outcomes and their associated payoffs and directionally how players should choose. And by examining the reasons behind the payoffs and why players would choose one move or another—recall that we must always ask ourselves why players should choose one path or another—we can get a sense for a game's dynamics. Compared with decision analysis exercises, we can get a great deal of useful and reliable game insights from base case numbers in Strategic Gaming projects because we tend to be more concerned with uncertainties posed by other players' moves rather than chance event uncertainties.

With both decision analysis and Strategic Gaming, we also want to engage in deterministic sensitivity analysis. As you'll recall, when we solicited probabilistic assessments for chance events, we determined a 10-50-90 range of values. Deterministic sensitivity involves a set of comparative static exercises in which one uses the economic model to estimate the outcomes at the low value of a chance event and then at the high value, leaving all other inputs at their base value. This yields low and high values for the model and the difference between the low and high values shows us how sensitive the model is to each input. A tornado diagram (see Figure 4.13) is a graphical representation of these outputs, showing which uncertainties have the most and least impact, in descending order, helping us to see which uncertainties are most important.[14]

This has two benefits in a Strategic Gaming exercise. One is that it helps us, as in decision analysis, understand what uncertainties should be part of a probabilistic analysis.

---

(14) For a fuller treatment of deterministic structuring and sensitivity, see McNamee and Celona, *Decision Analysis for the Professional,* pages 151-161, and Patrick Leach, *Why Can't You Just Give Me the Number?,* chapter 4.

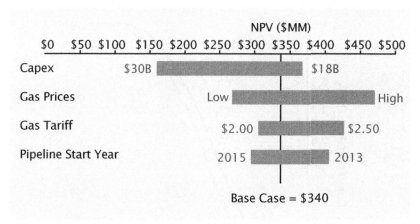

*Figure 4.13: Tornado Diagram*

The other is that it can give us insight into the risk factors that are of most import to other players in the game. Gaining such insight can be very useful as we think through tactical choices in an action plan. For instance, if we see that a competitor is subject to a big downside risk, we may be able to strike a favorable deal that mitigates the competitor's risk but transfers value to us.

After completing deterministic analysis, it is usually best to go one step further by considering the numbers probabilistically (or, as some might say, "risk" the numbers). Rather than use base case assumptions, we instead consider the entire range of possible values for each of the most important inputs (as revealed by the tornado diagram) and their associated probabilistic assessments. In the end, we calculate expected values for each outcome based on all the key uncertainties, and then analyze our game trees with those numbers.

As we work through our game trees and prune them to focus on certain outcomes that may be possible, it is often useful to take probabilistic analysis one step further and look at cumulative (probability) distributions. A cumulative distribution, also known as an s-curve, shows the probability that an outcome will be less than or equal to some value. So, for example, in Figure 4.14 we see the probability distribution in one outcome for four different players. The line that goes

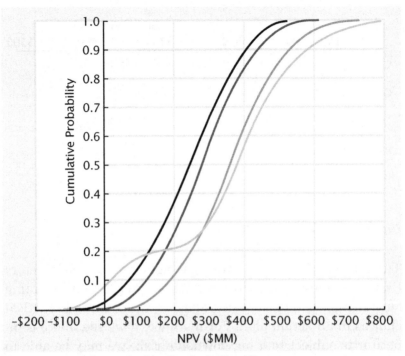

*Figure 4.14: Cumulative Probability Curves*

furthest to the left and right shows that the player represented by that line has a 10% chance of losing money, but approximately a 70% chance of capturing more value than the other three players. The other lines show players have only a very small or no chance of losing money, but their upside potential will not be as great as the first player.[15]

I typically run probabilistic analysis on only a few select outcomes in a game tree. The computational requirements are significant, particularly since there are choices by a number of players. Indeed, software packages in the public domain are not set up to run such game-theoretic analyses naturally. Moreover, it is not essential. If one has done a thorough game analysis, and narrowed potential outcomes, sufficient insight should be gained by building s-curves for a small, select number of outcomes.

---

(15) Besides cumulative distributions, one might use related graphs, such as a probability density function, flying bars, or histograms.

Together, deterministic and probabilistic treatment of the numbers can generate very valuable insights. They enable us to ground our thinking in quantitative measures, and make risk factors and trade-offs explicit from each player's perspective. By gaining valuable insight into not only our own choices, but those of others, we can learn a great deal about how strategic choices and tactics we may employ can best influence other players. The numbers can therefore enable us to shape and play the game effectively.

## Closing Thoughts

With the first two stages of the Strategic Gaming process, Dynamic Framing and Strategy Evaluation, we develop a clear structure of action-reaction dynamics and an enhanced understanding of the value of our choices. In turn, we can better anticipate and gain insight into how to influence others effectively.

Executives who can see the chess board of business clearly and anticipate and understand the best moves to make in a complex, interactive environment will be better able to position their companies for success, just as a good chess player will best a poor one. To maximize the chance of success though, executives and their teams need to be able to think and act several moves ahead of others, and that requires alignment on a contingent action plan.

The next chapter addresses that issue in discussing the third and final stage of the process, Execution Planning, in which we put together the insights from the first two stages into a plan of action. It involves building on the analysis by considering ways we might try to change the game, developing a contingency plan for playing the game over time, and crafting the tactics that can best implement the strategy we seek to pursue. Strategic Gaming is not simply an abstract 35,000-foot strategy process. It is one that helps us develop and then complement high-level strategic choices with sea-level implementation details that enable us to effectively influence others.

*"Part of the culture was a tendency to debate and argue and raise every issue to the highest level of abstraction. The process almost became one of the elegance of the definition of the problem rather than the actual execution of an action plan."*
*– Louis Gerstner, former CEO of IBM,*
*on what he saw upon coming to IBM*

# 5

# Execution Planning

In an IBM television commercial that aired several years ago, an executive entered a conference room and held up a thick report, proclaiming to his managers, "Here it is. Top-shelf consultants. Two million bucks. Pure strategic thinking. This could put us years ahead. The board is psyched. I'm psyched. It's a brilliant plan. One question: Given our current technology, is this implementable?" Blank stares and shaking heads indicated a disappointing no.

Although IBM's purpose was to show the value of its combination of business consulting and hardware, software, and IT services, one can question business strategy delivered by most consulting firms even when the technology is not essential (as it usually is not). Most strategy work ignores implementation because it is at the 35,000-foot level, considers tactics to be unimportant, and does not consider other players and how they may be influenced. Though many consultants claim to help clients embrace uncertainty, the behavior of other players is seldom treated with any degree of seriousness or rigor.

Yet to the extent we can anticipate and influence other players (rather than throw up our hands and declare their actions to be unpredictable), we can go a long way toward shaping our own destiny. To the extent we do not, we risk being outmaneuvered and marginalized.

Execution Planning, the third and final stage of the Strategic Gaming process, focuses on the need to address implementation in a way that specifies, over time and under possible contingencies, strategic moves and complementary tactics. To this point in the process, we will have discovered useful insights and discussed a variety of strategic moves and tactics that could be pursued. However, the findings have not been pulled together into a dynamic road map that details a sequential plan of action with clearly identifiable signposts, contingent moves, and tactics. That is the basic task and goal of this part of the process. Doing so also provides learning about, and is a valuable check on, the practicality and feasibility of alternative strategies. Indeed, the development of a dynamic road map that is both strategic and tactical can lead us to wisely pursue a strategy that is more do-able than one that, on the surface, appears to be more valuable.

## Changing the Game

Before we can develop a robust dynamic road map, we need to verify whether we have looked at all possible angles for the situation at hand. If we do this, we can ensure that we will have a robust, dynamic strategy. If we do not, we risk being blindsided.

We should therefore consider alternative assumptions about the structure of the games we have analyzed to see how robust our results are under a variety of assumptions and whether there may be a better strategy. Our initial games are the start of our analysis, and will give rise to thoughts about other possible games we may be playing. We might look at different sequences of play, other moves that we and others may have, other players that might be brought into the game, or a different business model. There are many possibilities, and our games are a tool that can facilitate brainstorming about game-changing ideas.

This will be particularly important if, in the evaluation of our initial games, we find that we are in a weak position that requires a game changer to realize success. Even if we do not appear to be in a weak position, it may be important to consider potential game changers our competitors can pursue to avoid being blindsided. Hence, we should ask not only about game changers for ourselves, but what sorts of actions other players could take that would really change the game. Doing so can help us avoid being the victim of unexpected actions from other players that can endanger the value of our strategic choices.

In crafting and evaluating a new set of games, we are essentially refining our Strategy Evaluation stage work. This is essential to have a more complete and insightful understanding of the situation. If our results are largely consistent in the fuller set of games, then we will have confidence that our findings are robust. Thus, if we find that we are going to be in a difficult position under a variety of potential scenarios, it may be prudent to exit, but if we consistently find that we are strongly positioned, that should provide confidence to proceed. If results vary under different assumptions, the analysis gives us insight into the type of game we should try to play and the actions necessary to shape the game in our favor.

## Developing Tactics

How the game is perceived by other stakeholders may be very important to realizing the best outcomes. This will be particularly true if we find that alternative structuring of the game gives rise to different results. In these cases, it is especially important to develop and employ tactics to shape others' perceptions so that they see the game as we prefer them to see it. Yet even if we see generally consistent and positive results with various assumptions in our game analysis, it may still be very important to frame the game for others to ensure they do what is in their own interest (as well as ours). It is possible, for example, that others may not recognize a win-win that our game-theoretic analysis has uncovered, and we would have to reveal the game to them. After all, other players will probably not have structured "the game" and will probably not see the implications of moves and countermoves as clearly as we have.

Exactly what tactics should we employ to best frame the game for other players? This depends on the situation and a variety of factors, but what is important is that we step outside the game and its basic strategic choices to think about the nitty-gritty tactical details that will best supplement and complement strategic choices. The tactics should follow from an understanding of our and others' strategic interests and alternatives, and the relevant uncertainties. With the structure of the games, and by understanding what is in it for others, we can come up with tactics that complement our optimal strategies. By understanding the logic of the interactions, the risks, trade-offs, the values at stake, and the menu of choices available to ourselves and others, we can have a more effective conversation with other players or figure out how to influence others through our actions. Tactics are thus built from an understanding of the strategic factors at work, and should be designed to supplement and complement the strategic choices we make.

This approach is in sharp contrast with common practice. I have found that many executives and negotiators (and even negotiation gurus!) believe tactics are the key to getting a good agreement and otherwise influencing others. They will try to convince other players without a sufficient understanding of the other players' perspectives and the range of win-win alternatives, believing that their skills in persuasion can lead them to success. As a result, they do not have a proper appreciation for what tactics can work and what probably will not work. All too often they unsuccessfully try to "spin" another player into doing something they should not want to do.

This is a misguided approach for at least three reasons:

♦ It is prone to failure because the tactical emphasis will neglect to clearly see what is in it for the other party and how to best reach a win-win solution. Countless hours are spent "running into brick walls" or seeing "two ships pass in the night."

♦ When it succeeds, it can create a win-lose scenario that can jeopardize the future of a relationship and may be ethically questionable.

♦ Since the approach is often based on gut instincts rather than careful analysis, the tactical emphasis can easily delude deal makers into believing an agreement is good when in fact it will result in winner's curse.

All in all then, tactics are important for successful implementation, but they should not replace sound strategic thinking. Tactics should supplement and complement choices we make based on an analysis of the strategic situation.

Tactics can take several forms, such as:

♦ Educational tactics
♦ Psychological tactics
♦ Eliciting information
♦ Credible commitments and signaling.

Educational and psychological tactics can be used to convince others to take a particular course of action. Tactics may also be designed to elicit information from others, thereby helping us to reduce our uncertainties about other players. Other tactics are useful to establish credibility. Of course, there is often overlap between these different types of tactics, and it may be advisable to employ more than one.

*Educational tactics.* In many cases, it is important to let other players know about the nature of the game. After all, other players have probably not thought through the structure and implications of the action-reaction dynamics as clearly as you have with a Strategic Gaming exercise. As such, others will be particularly subject to natural limitations on processing information objectively.

When we are seeking a win-win partnership with another player it is often important to reveal the game, showing why it is in another's interest to take particular actions that lead to joint gains. Even in competitive situations it may be important to reveal the game; it may be a way to deter or dissuade a competitor from taking actions that would lead to mutual losses. In other cases, it may be important to selectively educate others—advise them of certain issues, but not others—to influence them effectively. There are thus many situations in which the standard reflex to conceal information may be more dangerous than openness.

*Psychological tactics.* Game theory is based on an assumption of economic rationality in which players are deemed to maximize their expected value. However, no game theorist would say that people are completely rational; psychological factors often preclude such behavior. The rationality assumption is useful as a first cut, and psychological factors can then be considered and used to great effect. As Nobel laureate Thomas Schelling writes in *The Strategy of Conflict*, "we seriously restrict ourselves by the assumption of rational behavior," and "the results we reach under this constraint may prove to be either a good approximation of reality or a caricature. Any abstraction runs a risk of this sort, and we have to be prepared to use judgment with any results we reach." Nonetheless, he contends "the assumption of rational behavior is a productive one" and we should "view our results as a bench mark for further approximation to reality." Indeed, he argues, "the assumption that the participants coolly and 'rationally' calculate their advantages according to a consistent value system forces us to think more thoroughly about the meaning of 'irrationality.'"[1]

Schelling's profound points are highly relevant to the nature and practice of Strategic Gaming. We start with the rationality assumption to gain insights, but then need to step outside the game to think about the tactics necessary for effective execution of a plan. With a "rational" game-theoretic

(1) Schelling, *The Strategy of Conflict*, pages 4 and 16.

analysis complete, we can most effectively draw on psychological considerations.

One particularly appropriate psychological tactic comes from studies that explicitly challenge game theory and other economic tools and theories. Daniel Kahneman, a Nobel laureate in Economics in 2002, and Amos Tversky demonstrated in experimental studies that the framing of a problem (its description) is crucially important to how people make decisions, contrary to theories of expected-utility maximization that underpin the decision sciences and economics (including game theory). In particular, they showed that individuals seem to be more averse to losses, relative to a reference level, than partial to gains of the same size. How a decision is framed can affect whether people are risk-seeking or risk-averse.[2]

The implication of this is that when one wants to exploit another's possible risk-aversion, it could be useful to emphasize potential losses. Here is where our quantitative work ties in. With drill downs like tornados, we can understand what the hot-button risk factors are and focus on those in framing a decision for another player.

In other projects, I have found individuals' egos to be an issue. For instance, in one engagement with a small alternative energy company, we followed the Strategic Gaming process and developed a contingency plan. Much of this drew on tactical discussions about how to make a deal with the owner of a rival company who appeared to have a big ego and appeared to be willing to lose a substantial amount of his own money by dragging out a controversy with my client. Yet doing so would, with near certainty, result in the rival losing in court. My client did not want those delays and was willing to make a deal; an agreement made a lot of sense for both parties, but was not going to be easy given the rival owner's disposition. We discussed how to make the game clear to the rival's owner. My client would show him how he would ultimately lose in court, and juxtapose that with the alternative of making a

(2) Amos Tversky and Daniel Kahneman, "Rational Choice and the Framing of Decisions," in Hogarth and Reder (eds.), *Rational Choice: The Contrast between Economics and Psychology,* pages 67-84.

deal quickly with my client. This was an education effort to prevent ego from getting in the way of rational decision making. Combined with this, there would be a psychological effort to exploit potential risk-aversion, as per Kahneman and Tversky, by emphasizing how much the rival owner could lose. If necessary, my client could then offer sweeter deals, up to a point, comparing the gains to the large losses that would be suffered by the rival owner if he did not accept. If all of this failed, my client would then wait for a court date.

As this suggests, carrying out such tactics is not always easy and may not always succeed, no matter how well executed. But at least we will have given it a strong and sensible effort, and will have contingency plans in place to ensure ultimate success, even if not the best and most immediate outcome.

One word of caution about using psychological tactics is in order. Many are tempted to push the psychological route early and often. We should always keep in mind that while psychological and other tactics are important, they should follow sound strategic analysis. They should supplement and complement strategic choices, not replace them, and be based on an understanding of other players' perspectives. While psychological factors are omnipresent, executives in most companies usually try to be economically rational even though they are seldom, if ever, completely rational.

With large and small companies in a variety of industries, I have found time and again that competitors, partners, and other players deemed by my clients to be exhibiting irrational behavior were shown through Strategic Gaming analysis to have been acting quite rationally. Because they had not yet thought through the game, my clients failed to adequately understand the other players' drivers and alternatives. If my clients had acted on their initial judgments about others' ir-rationality, they would probably have made costly decisions. Fortunately, they used Strategic Gaming.

*Eliciting information.* A common refrain of executives is, "If we knew more about that player's drivers, we could make a better choice." One of the insights Strategic Gaming typi-cally provides is clarity about others' drivers and their likely choices. At times, though, there will still be uncertainty. In those cases, Strategic Gaming typically provides us with clues about what uncertainties are important; it helps us narrow down the scope of potential uncertainties we should care about. This provides insight into how we might elicit information—that is, what questions to ask, and how.

Drawing on such insights, I usually like to work with my clients to develop a list of specific questions that are designed to elicit a great deal of information. Some questions may be designed so that a lack of response is a clear signal about where another player is coming from. In my experience, and that of my clients, asking the right sorts of questions can elicit a lot more information than otherwise seemed obtainable.

The exercise should also give us an idea of who to query. One might directly question a player, but it might be better to ask another player questions that help us understand the player in question indirectly. Another indirect way to elicit information from a player is to take an action in the market that is designed to evoke a telling response. For example, making a public statement about one's intention to do something could provoke a response or non-response that is quite informative.

Direct interaction with other players may be useful for influencing others by "planting seeds" in their heads. For instance, one project team was unsure whether another player was soon going to make an offer on an asset the client coveted, and what time frame the seller had in mind for accepting an offer. By making inquiries with the seller, we might learn some or all of what we wanted to know. We would also show a level of interest that would probably impel the seller to lengthen its time frame for accepting bids, thus providing us with a useful delay.

A conversation may also have the simultaneous effect of educating another player and helping to establish credibility. In one project, the team had been frustrated with their inability to influence a partner. We decided that the issue of concern needed to be elevated to a higher level, both within the client organization and the partner's. A top executive from the client would have to have a conversation with his counterpart to hear why the partner had been reluctant to proceed more aggressively. He would also let the partner know why we thought there was significant value in a bolder investment. If we continued to meet resistance, the contingency plan called for us to pursue some tough actions, including the vetoing of ongoing production plans. If we got to that point, our commitment to be tough would be more credible. The partner would be more likely to believe our threats to be serious because the issue had been raised from a high level six months prior.

One should note, finally, that attempts to elicit information or educate others could tip our hand in a detrimental way. Hence, a common concern discussed in Strategic Gaming engagements is whether, by seeking or sharing information, we create a less advantageous situation.

*Credible commitments and signaling.* Though credibility and signaling have been mentioned in various places throughout this book, it is important to consider a fuller range of tactics that may be employed in order to enhance credibility. Success of many influence strategies requires us to convince others that we will come through on the commitments we make.

Individuals and companies make two broad types of commitments where credibility is important: promises to do something, and threats to retaliate. To make promises or threats believable to the point that others will be influenced effectively, we must be willing and able to bind ourselves, and be able to communicate that to another player. To be sure, we may successfully bluff by creating a perception that we are probably committed to a particular course of action. Nonetheless, for maximum credibility "we must," as Schelling writes, "leave as little room as possible for judgment or discretion in carrying out the threat."[3]

In what ways might we enhance credibility? Putting our reputation on the line is one way. John Kennedy's televised speech during the Cuban Missile Crisis, in which he demanded that Nikita Khrushchev remove the weapons from Cuba, was an effort by the American president to put his personal politi-

---

(3) Schelling, *The Strategy of Conflict*, page 40.

cal reputation on the line to signal to the Soviet leader his determination to see the missiles removed. To back down from such a public threat would be political suicide. Similarly, CEOs sometimes make public commitments that they are forging ahead with a particular strategy in order to deter competitors and influence other players.

Seldom, however, is it possible for such commitments to be thoroughly binding. They almost always have some wiggle room. Hence, what is also important is an individual's or company's starting point–the reputation one brings to the table. The reputation question is very important in developing signaling tactics. A proper assessment of one's reputation (from others' perspectives) is crucial to understanding how much or little wiggle room is needed to give a commitment sufficient credibility so that it will have the desired effect on others. Of course, quantification of games and associated analysis help us make such assessments with a degree of objectivity.

In some cases, our reputation may be so weak that there is no way to credibly signal. Or we might find that, to overcome our reputation for weakness, we must make such a strong commitment that we would incur unacceptably high costs. In still other cases, our strong reputation may make only lower levels of commitment necessary.

Because reputation carries a great deal of weight in the credibility of commitments and other signals, Strategic Gaming projects also consider how our actions in a particular situation will impact our ability to effectively make credible commitments at future points in time. While we should be cautious to not overemphasize the impact of our actions over time and under different circumstances, the signals we are sending (or the lack thereof) can have a strong, long-term impact on our reputation and, in turn, our ability to influence others. This should be taken into consideration.

Another tactic is to take preemptive action that locks us into a course of action and creates a credible commitment designed to deter a competitor. By foregoing the power to retreat, both we and our competitor would suffer damage if the competitor were not deterred. This was a tactic considered in a project I once worked. The client was seeking to build an offshore natural gas plant that would use a pipeline to ship gas to power plants onshore. The problem was that two other companies wanted to do the same, and in all likelihood only one plant could be profitable. We considered initiating construction on part of the pipeline that would be needed to pipe gas onshore, which would cost tens of millions of dollars. Along with a public statement of our commitment to the project, this action would go a long way toward relinquishing our ability to retreat and help dissuade our competitors from going down a mutually damaging path.

Another tactic that helps show strength is, paradoxically, to convince others of our weakness. If, for instance, we can persuade others that our hands are tied due to organizational constraints, others will be more apt to believe we are committed to a particular path. Or, we might argue that a partner will not allow us to make an agreement. I have found this to be a tactic that companies in joint ventures can and do make toward governments with which they are negotiating. Weakness can thus make a signal credible because of its power to bind.

## Building a Dynamic Road Map

A key benefit of working to develop a set of tactics is that we can learn something about the feasibility of strategies. If in our tactical discussions we realize that it is going to be very difficult to implement tactics that are an essential complement to a strategy, we will need to develop a different set of choices. If we do not think through the tactics, we will not fully appreciate the practicalities of a given strategy, and could go down a costly path.

This will become especially clear as we pull our strategic and tactical insights together into a detailed, contingent plan of action. These dynamic road maps help guide a team's actions to enable effective execution. They outline the strategic choices and tactical moves a team should implement to shape the game

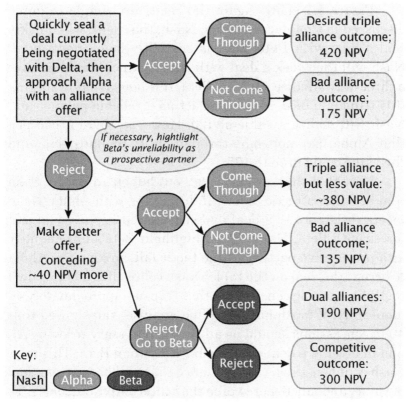

*Figure 5.1: Dynamic Road Map*

and to efficiently and effectively respond to signposts—events and other players' actions—over time.

I usually try to use a flow chart diagram, as in Figure 5.1, but dynamic road maps can take a variety of forms. Some may prefer to use game trees or schematic game trees that identify the paths to take and tactics that will best complement the choices. Others may prefer a Gantt chart style. In other cases, I have found it sufficient to simply describe the strategic choices and tactics in words. Whatever format is chosen, the action plan should clearly specify strategic moves, tactics, and signposts that can lead us to change direction in the near-term and over time. It is often a good idea to also show the value at stake with different choices and outcomes so that decision makers can see the potential upside and downside of alternative courses of action.

Figure 5.1 shows again the relatively simple example discussed in Chapter 2. In this, Nash, the client, will quickly seal a deal with Delta that is currently being negotiated. Nash will then seek a deal with Alpha, which would finalize a three-way alliance vis-à-vis Beta. It is hoped that by forging this triple alliance, Alpha will act as a reliable partner and Nash will realize a value of 420. However, there is concern that Alpha may not come through on its commitments and the value could drop to 175.

Note that there is also a call out bubble in the diagram that specifies a tactic to use. If, in talking with Alpha, Nash meets resistance to a deal and senses that Alpha could join forces with Beta, Nash should highlight Beta's unreliability as a prospective partner. If the tactic fails to convince Alpha to accept the deal on the table, Nash could offer a better deal to Alpha, making concessions that transfer approximately 40 more in NPV to Alpha. The game analysis had showed that 40 in concessions should be all that is necessary to swing Alpha in favor of a deal with Nash rather than Beta. This way, Nash could ensure a triple alliance that still has a great deal of value, and much more value than alternative outcomes. To concede more would leave value on the table unnecessarily.

Of course, if things do not work out and Nash finds itself in an alliance with Delta that competed with an Alpha-Beta alliance, the outcome would be substantially worse (190) than a well-functioning triple alliance (380 to 420). Seeing this, Nash decision makers may be willing to concede more than 40 if they meet resistance from Alpha. Indeed, if Alpha thought through the game well they would see that Nash's walk away point should be much higher and would make this point to Nash. Indeed, Nash should be willing to offer Alpha not 40, but rather up to 230, the difference between the 420 triple alliance outcome and the 190 dual alliance outcome.

In conversations with Alpha, Nash executives would need to make assessments about how likely it was that Alpha and Beta would get together and, more generally, why Alpha may be showing resistance to a deal with Nash. Has Alpha thought through the game and figured out that it can extract more value from Nash? Or does Alpha believe the value of an alliance with Beta to be greater than Nash believes it to be? Or is it possible Alpha believes that going it alone in a competitive environment is best? Understanding Alpha's viewpoint is essential to understanding how far Nash decision makers should be willing to go in making concessions to Alpha.

Typically, dynamic road maps for projects are much more intricate. In fact, sometimes my colleagues and I also find it helpful to supplement the flow chart, Gantt chart or other dynamic road map with a detailed write-up on key issues, such as specific talking points for discussions with other players or explicit instructions for team members to follow in their external interactions. In some cases, this can be very important, as saying the wrong thing could completely undermine a strategy. Often it is also useful to include payoffs to other players in several places. To know what is in it for another player can prove useful in implementation and may help management understand the validity of a proposed approach. This is particularly the case in detailing negotiation strategies and tactics.

It may also be useful to highlight open questions for decision makers. In many cases, there will be particular decisions in an action plan for which a project team does not feel comfortable making a recommendation. Leaving these as open questions for decision makers and providing clear information on the issues and trade-offs involved in each decision can be very useful for helping management reach a decision and settling on a plan of action.

## Ensuring Alignment

The foregoing suggests that it is essential to ensure alignment in this stage of the process. The beauty of Strategic Gaming is that even though it surfaces many counterintuitive insights, alignment is facilitated by the nature of the process. Everyone on a project team adopts the same language and logic from the beginning of the process, so even if team members come to the project with much different views, almost invariably the process enables them to reach alignment on the most complex of issues.

This has often been the case even when the results differed sharply from team members' original perspectives. Sometimes at the beginning of a project I have team members write down their views on what the company's strategy should be and place their responses in a sealed envelope. When we open the envelopes at the project's conclusion, the differences in where we ended up and what team members wrote is invariably astounding. And yet, those who participated in the envelope exercise never have a problem with where we ended up and see the value of Strategic Gaming. The logic and quantitative rigor of Strategic Gaming helps project teams work through the implications of their assumptions and come to more sophisticated and better conclusions than they otherwise would.

The foregoing also suggests that alignment with higher level decision makers is very important, and getting alignment with management can be more difficult since they may not have participated extensively in the process. Moreover, management may have broader or somewhat different concerns than those of a project team. Nonetheless, the logic of Strategic Gaming is straightforward and intuitive. Even when the results are highly counterintuitive, the broad scope and structure and quantitative rigor of Strategic Gaming exercises help make results compelling. Hence, decision makers typically have no problem understanding why a project team that used Strategic Gaming came to the results it did. They find their questions answered with valuable and valid insights that give rise to a sensible, intelligent discussion and an implementable plan of action.

## Conclusion

We have now discussed the three stages of the Strategic Gaming process. The first stage, Dynamic Framing, is for mapping out the potential interactions and learning events, helping us to see the structure of the game and make valuable qualitative insights. The Strategy Evaluation stage builds on this structure to develop an economic model and populate game trees with value measures for each of the key players so that we can undertake a quantitative analysis of the games and determine our and others' optimal strategic choices. The final stage, Execution Planning, addresses implementation issues. By looking at ways we and others may change the game and developing tactics as part of a dynamic road map, we can build alignment on a robust strategy for shaping and playing the game of business.

Although the Strategic Gaming process tends to take a broader scope than most other strategy approaches, it is remarkably efficient. Time and again clients have told me that they achieved a better, fuller analysis in a matter of weeks than they had in three, six, or even twelve months of work. Strategic Gaming gets to the right issues quickly and enables executives to see the essence of interactive situations clearly. Executives come to understand the alternatives and value at stake, not only from their perspective, but from those of other players. This provides tremendous insight into how to influence others. Used proactively, Strategic Gaming can help executives shape the game they are in before things really get going. When executives are in a bind and turn to Strategic Gaming, the results help them see how they might change the game to their advantage.

Although Strategic Gaming is not a crystal ball or a magic wand, it does help reduce uncertainties about other players substantially, enabling executives to take actions to influence other players effectively and avoid being blindsided. Strategic Gaming has consistently empowered executives to capture great value in a range of industries—including oil and gas, alternative energy, high tech, pharmaceuticals, electric power, and financial services—and for a variety of topics, including competitive risk decisions, alliance and joint venture strategy, mergers and acquisitions and licensing negotiations, procurement, and political risk. The three chapters that follow discuss some of these cases to illustrate the power of Strategic Gaming.

# Part III: Strategic Gaming in Action: Examples

*"In this life, the big, strong guys are always taking from the smaller, weaker guys, but ... the smart take from the strong"*
– Pete Carril, legendary Princeton basketball coach, in The Smart Take from the Strong, *quoting his father's advice*

# 6

# Coordination Games

Strategic Gaming has helped astute executives capture billions of dollars of value on a wide range of business strategy issues. This and the next two chapters review some example cases to illustrate the process at work and its potential benefits.

Since the work my colleagues and I do with Strategic Gaming tends to be highly confidential, the cases discussed below are disguised. Company names, and sometimes the industry, are not revealed, and some details are altered to protect client interests. Nonetheless, the cases and results are real and demonstrate the power of Strategic Gaming to generate valuable insights and capture significant value in the face of difficult but common business dilemmas.

The cases reviewed are organized around the three types of game situations discussed in chapter 2: Coordination, Collaboration, and Competition (the "3Cs"). All game situations fit somewhere in the 3C space and typically have one of the 3Cs as the predominant feature (see Figure 6.1). That said,

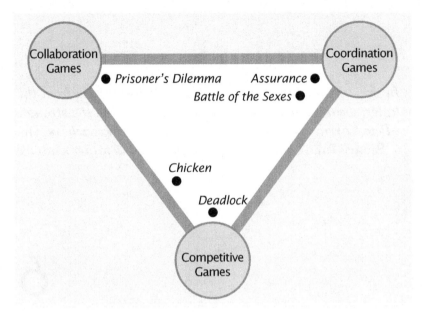

*Figure 6.1: The "3 Cs"*

we should be cognizant of the fact that real-world business issues seldom fit perfectly into one corner of the 3C triangle. A coordination problem, for example, may also be characterized by competitive or collaborative dilemmas.

Consider contractual negotiations. They take place because two parties see win-win potential, and the parties will haggle over the terms (i.e., which win-win outcome is best). Yet many contracts will also have provisions that punish parties for reneging on terms in order to overcome collaboration dilemmas, and they may have non-compete clauses to minimize competitive concerns. Hence, forcing a real world problem into a single archetype may lead to an oversimplification or mischaracterization of the situation and to misguided prescriptions. Nonetheless, since different issues have one of the 3Cs as the predominant feature, it is a useful distinction for the case discussion and for considering whether problems you face could benefit from Strategic Gaming.

Coordination games are characterized by a win-win opportunity, while deviation from an agreement by any of the players will result in a lose-lose situation. Negotiations are typically about trying to reach an agreement on a perceived win-win solution, and so are coordination issues first and foremost. Hence, I focus on such cases below.

## Negotiations with a Powerful Supplier

Nash Industries' assets in a particular region needed to be serviced regularly with a particular piece of equipment, which we'll call "Asset Helper," and with a level of competence only a few suppliers could provide. Over the years, one particular supplier of Asset Helper, Black Dog, developed a near-monopoly position with Nash for work on these assets. With the position of Black Dog in servicing Nash solidifying, the supplier had been raising its prices regularly, and over the previous three years rates had increased 75%. Now the Nash team was faced with a demand for another increase of 15%.

Nash had been happy with Black Dog's work, but acrimony and mistrust had developed, in large part because of the repeated price increases. There was a concern that the worsening relations could jeopardize the quality of service that Black Dog provided. For its part, Black Dog insisted the rate increases were justified because there was a serious labor shortage. Black Dog executives argued it was very difficult to find sufficiently qualified labor to meet the work needs and requirements of the job. Nash felt it was at the mercy of Black Dog. With the labor shortage and few other suppliers who could step in and do the work, Nash felt it was in a very difficult position. Could Nash do something to negotiate a deal better than what Black Dog put on the table, or did Nash have to cave now and in the future?

We structured the game much like most negotiations should be structured. As shown in the game tree in Figure 6.2, we took as the starting point Black Dog's 15% rate increase demand and Nash's choices were simply to accept or reject the demand. Later on we could refine this simple distinction and think about counteroffers less than 15%. But for now, accept and reject would be sufficient for the initial analysis.

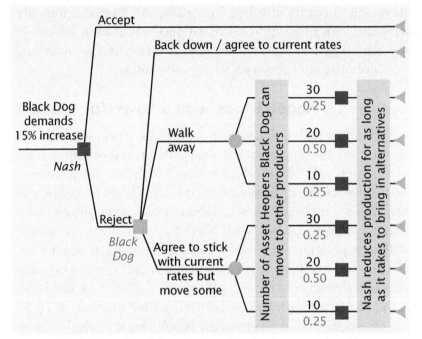

*Figure 6.2: Supplier Negotiation Game*

If Nash rejected the rate increase, Black Dog had three choices modeled in the game tree:

♦ Black Dog could back down and agree to the current rates,

♦ At the other extreme, Black Dog could walk away from doing business with Nash entirely, pulling all Asset Helpers from service to Nash, or

♦ Black Dog could agree to stick with the current rates, but move some of its Asset Helpers to other producers at the higher rate.

In developing the game tree, we realized there was an important issue that was not previously appreciated. It was not clear that Black Dog could simply place its Asset Helpers with other companies. In fact, most other companies used a different version of Asset Helper ("Asset Helper Turbo"), and outside this particular region the use of Asset Helper was limited. Hence, from a qualitative standpoint, we realized that Nash may have some leverage.

To quantify this and to reach a deeper understanding of the potential leverage, we had to ask how many Black Dog Asset Helpers supplied to Nash could be placed with other producers who might need them. We worked with the client team to make an uncertainty assessment (a 10-50-90 range for the number of Asset Helpers Black Dog could move at the increased rates). We decided that 10 was a reasonable minimum, 30 the maximum, and 20 the most likely case. As Black Dog had 70 units in service with Nash, it was clear that Black Dog could not simply walk away from doing business with Nash without shooting itself in the foot. If Black Dog decided to stick with the current rates but move some Asset Helpers to others to get higher rates, they might move 10 to 30. Nash might suffer, as some production would be lost temporarily since there would not be an immediate replacement of any Asset Helpers that were moved. It would take some time to bring in alternative suppliers.

We then created a simple economic model from both Nash's and Black Dog's perspectives to understand the value to each player in the different game outcomes shown in the game tree. The results were quite intriguing, and the graphs in Figure 6.3 do a nice job in portraying the results. Quite counter intuitively, Nash would actually make money if Black Dog pulled 10, 20, or 30 Asset Helpers. Indeed, Black Dog would have to pull a little more than 40 Asset Helpers before Nash would lose money! The reason is that Nash would be able to bring in other suppliers over time. While Nash might lose some production until replacement suppliers were on the job, and that would have a cost, Nash would not be paying Black Dog for the Asset Helpers that were pulled and would bring in new suppliers at a better rate. The net effect was that Nash would actually make money. Nash could thus stand firm, and would not be bluffing.

For Black Dog, meanwhile, there was not a credible threat of exit. If Black Dog were to pull all of its Asset Helpers, it would lose money unless more than 40 Asset Helpers could be placed with other companies at the higher price demanded. However, we estimated that Black Dog could only pull and

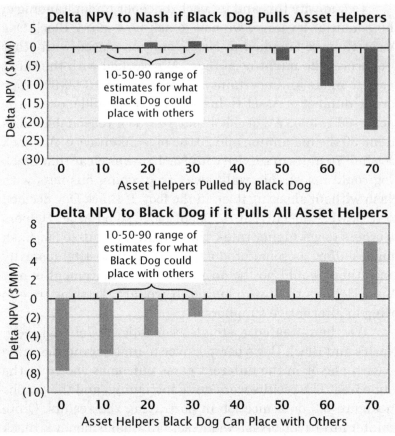

*Figure 6.3: Value Perspectives: Nash and Black Dog*

place as many as 30 Asset Helpers. Black Dog thus stood to lose quite a bit of money by taking a hard line position and coming through on the threat. We were therefore convinced that if Black Dog took a hard line position, it was a bluff. If Black Dog could and did move some of the Asset Helpers away from Nash in order to get higher prices elsewhere, that would be fine for Nash. Nash would not take a financial hit; in fact Nash would improve its NPV a bit. Nash would also be reducing Black Dog's monopoly power by bringing in other suppliers, thus changing the situation from one in which it was beholden to a monopoly supplier to one in which there were several suppliers that could provide the services. Nash would be creating more of a market, which would help keep prices down over the longer term.

The recommendation then was for Nash to stand firm. Nash should tell Black Dog that it would not agree to rate increases and that if Black Dog wanted to take some of its business elsewhere, that would be fine. We were confident that Black Dog did not have strong alternatives. Nash did not need to feel like it was at the mercy of Black Dog. To the contrary, Black Dog was at the mercy of Nash, for it did not have a credible threat of exit. Although a highly counterintuitive set of recommendations was developed (when compared with where the team was at the project's start), the Strategic Gaming analysis made the results clear and powerful. Nash did not have to accede to the demand for a 15% rate increase on a spend that was in the tens of millions of dollars annually, and in so doing also leveled the playing field with Black Dog.

Nash now understood that it could, over the long term, change the landscape with regard to its suppliers of Asset Helper. Nash could start to bring in other suppliers while taking a strong position with Black Dog. The current monopoly supplier situation could be transformed into one with more diversity in competition. Pricing would be closer to that of a market. No longer would Nash feel that it would have to be a price taker. Hence, the team set out to negotiate longer term pricing arrangements with suppliers that would help vitiate the need for regular negotiations that wasted time and led to a very acrimonious and inefficient situation. Less time and energy would be spent on negotiations that produced no benefit, while operations would see a significant efficiency gain.

## Negotiation of a Pharmaceutical Marketing Agreement

Nash Pharmaceuticals had a promising new drug in its pipeline but had limited sales and marketing capability. To get adequate value out of its product, it needed to make a deal with another company that could effectively market the drug.

Analysis on prospective partners concluded that one company, Green Dog, was clearly the most appropriate for

marketing Nash's drug. Nash then used Strategic Gaming
to understand the value of different deal structures with
Green Dog. It was important to understand how Green Dog's
incentives under different deal structures would influence
its actions and thus the success of marketing Nash's drug.
We needed to know how to design a win-win agreement that
would provide the greatest possible value for Nash, and how
to persuade Green Dog to agree to such a deal.

Green Dog was an appealing partner because it already
had marketed a similar product of its own with great success.
For Nash's product to be successful, it would likely need Green
Dog's drug to be cannibalized. Thus, Green Dog needed a win-
win deal in which it would have an incentive to cannibalize
its own product in favor of Nash's (to a significant degree at
least). These negotiations would be somewhat involved, so
there needed to be a good strategic and tactical plan of action
for the negotiations.

We set out to look at different possible agreements and
compare those against one another and with the alternative
possibility of no agreement, which would mean that Nash
would have to go it alone and market the drug itself. Without
looking at the possibility of no agreement, we would not know
what the win-win space is. I think about the win-win space,
illustrated simply in Figure 6.4, as bounded on one side by
what I call the walk away point, the point at which the player

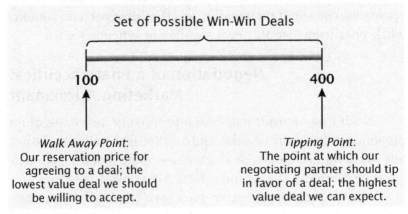

*Figure 6.4: The Win-Win Space*

doing the analysis (in this case, Nash) would walk away from a deal. On the other end is what I call the tipping point, the minimal point at which the other player would tip in favor of a deal. This is simply the other player's walk away point. It is important to consider both the walk away and tipping points to understand the win-win space, and each player should want to get as close to the other player's walk away point (the tipping point) as possible.[1] In this case, while Nash could not market the drug as effectively on its own, it could probably still make money on the product, and we would want to consider how that profitability compared with partnering deals Nash could make with Green Dog. Also, for Green Dog the issue is potentially important as well, as certain partnering deals may be better than competing against Nash.

The first option we looked at in the game tree of Figure 6.5 shows that Nash could go it alone or offer terms that copy those in a prior marketing agreement that Green Dog had done well with on another product. In the game tree, Green Dog can accept or reject the offer. If the offer is rejected, that would be equivalent to Nash going it alone. If the offer is accepted, Green Dog then has a choice to cannibalize its own drug in favor of Nash's or to promote both drugs simultaneously without giving primacy to Nash's drug. While this possibility might not be completely consistent with the terms of the agreement, it would be difficult for Nash to monitor and do anything about it.

Analyzing this game tree, we saw that both Nash and Green Dog could get more value out of this partnership with cannibalization of the existing drug ($400 MM and $1000 MM) than if Nash goes it alone and the two compete with

---

(1) The point at which a player should walk away from a deal is often referred to as a reservation price or what Roger Fisher, William Ury and Bruce Patton call the BATNA (Best Alternative To a Negotiated Agreement) in *Getting to Yes: Negotiating Agreement Without Giving In*, Second Edition. The difference here is that we are trying to understand not just our own BATNA, but that of the other player. This will define whether there is a win-win space and thus whether we should even want to get to "yes," for in some cases there is no win-win. It also helps us understand how far we can push our negotiating partner in reaching an agreement.

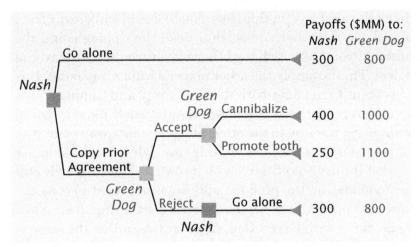

*Figure 6.5: Pharmaceutical Negotiation Game 1*

one another ($300 MM and $800 MM). However, Nash should prefer to go-it-alone under these terms because Green Dog has an incentive to promote both the new and existing drugs, which nets Green Dog $1100 MM, rather than cannibalize its own drug and get $1000 MM. And since Green Dog should promote both, Nash would be worse off ($250 MM) than if it went alone ($300 MM).

For a win-win deal, Green Dog needs concessions of more than $100 MM to ensure it will cannibalize, but if Nash gives up $100 MM in value, it gains nothing over the go-it-alone strategy. Nash, therefore, needs to find a better deal structure to open discussions with Green Dog, and if this particular contract design comes up, Nash will need to make it clear to Green Dog the deal structure bears unacceptable risks for Nash.

The game tree in Figure 6.6 is structurally similar, but in this case the underlying deal that would be offered has stronger incentives for Green Dog to cannibalize its own drug. Here we can see that Green Dog makes more money by cannibalizing ($900 MM) than by promoting both ($550 MM) and would rather accept this deal than compete with Nash ($800 MM). For Nash, cannibalization results in a significantly better outcome than going-it-alone ($500 MM versus $300 MM),

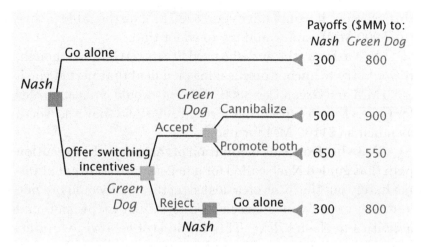

*Figure 6.6: Pharmaceutical Negotiation Game 2*

and is better than the $400 MM it would have gotten if Green Dog cannibalized under the initial contractual arrangement evaluated.

This deal structure is clearly a win-win that gives Nash substantially more value than the previous deal terms, without the partner risks, and about the same or more than other possible deals. Green Dog would get less than in the others but more than if Nash were to go-it-alone.

Before going into negotiations, we fine-tuned this structure to offer a deal that could capture even more value. In the deal as structured for our analysis, Nash would be leaving $100 MM on the table, the difference for Green Dog between $900 MM in the deal and $800 MM from dual competition. Hence, we wanted to find a deal that would raise Nash's value from the deal from $500 MM to $600 MM while lowering Green Dog's from $900 MM to $800 MM. This would be the starting point for Nash in negotiations, something that was a win-win but got Nash the best possible win-win. From there Nash could concede some value. How much? For Nash the value that could be conceded is up to the point at which Nash would wind up with the value it would get from a competitive outcome, $300 MM. What that further implies is that, if Green Dog had done this exercise, it would have seen $200 MM on the table (above the $900 MM), and would try to go for that.

As Nash was the one who used Strategic Gaming, though, it would try to anchor discussions on a deal that netted Nash $600 MM and Green Dog $800 MM. This would make it harder for Green Dog to expect that it could get a deal that was worth as much as $1100 MM for itself.

Drawing from this evaluation of the game, the execution plan that guided Nash called for a negotiation stance that immediately put the focus on a deal structure that would provide a strong incentive for Green Dog to switch its promotional activities to Nash's drug. This would still be a win-win that would fairly distribute risks and incentives and provide better value for Green Dog than a competitive situation.

If Green Dog were to ask for a deal structure similar to the one we first analyzed, Nash would be prepared to show that such a deal would create unacceptable risks, ones that would make Nash better off going it alone and competing with Green Dog. And for Green Dog, Nash would point out, competing would not be as valuable as the deal structure being offered.

To make this credible, Nash would need to convey a conviction that it would be able to market its drug effectively and compete with Green Dog. Nash not only needed to say that it would be willing to spend the money to do so, but would need to develop and reveal contingency plans to build its sales force and marketing capabilities. Nash would also point to its recent hiring and public announcements that it was committed to marketing the drug effectively. In addition, Nash would point to a strong track record in building competitive capabilities from scratch in the past. In other words, Nash would do everything it could to show that competing with Green Dog was a credible alternative, and one that should give Green Dog pause.

In the end, the strategy and tactics were highly effective in the negotiations. If Nash had agreed with what Green Dog most preferred or wound up competing, it would have realized an NPV hundreds of millions of dollars less than it got by getting agreement on a win-win deal that maximized the incentive for Green Dog to largely cannibalize its own drug.

*"A pessimist sees the difficulty in every opportunity;
an optimist sees the opportunity in every difficulty"*
*– Winston Churchill*

# 7

# Collaboration Games

Collaboration games are characterized by the possibility of a win-win, but also an incentive to deviate from an agreement to gain an advantage, such as we see in the Prisoner's Dilemma. Such games are the reason we have legally binding contracts, which are designed to ensure that each party to a contract lives up to its side of an agreement. Without such an enforcement mechanism, each party would have an incentive to deviate from the agreement. Knowing that, the parties would fail to reach an agreement in the first place and not realize a win-win outcome.

Joint ventures (JVs) are classic examples of collaboration, for two or more players create a formal structure for ensuring cooperation when they form a JV. Of course, in creating and maintaining a JV there are coordination issues as well, and the parties to a JV may have divergent interests in some respects as a result of competitive factors. Such issues are endemic in the oil and gas industry, for companies are often partnering with their competitors and competing with their partners, particularly in the upstream (exploration and production) side of the business in which companies typically partner on projects that cost billions of dollars. My colleagues and I have applied Strategic Gaming extensively in many oil and gas JV cases, one of which is discussed below.

## Gaining Alignment in an Oil & Gas JV

Nash Oil held a one-third equity stake in an oil field called "Charlie Brown." The operator of the field, Red Dog, also had a one-third stake, and four other partners made up the balance. Nash was trying to get Red Dog to agree to a more aggressive drilling program to tap potential reserves that Nash geologists believed to hold significant value. For months, Red Dog refused to agree, and the other partners were thought to be reluctant to spend more CAPEX to develop the field further.

In working on this case, my colleagues first did economic analysis to understand the potential value of developing the field given different technical alternatives. For the commercial side, we used Strategic Gaming to make sure that we could get the right sort of win-win with our JV partner Red Dog and the other partners in the Charlie Brown field. Here we looked at what choices we had and whether they could be effective levers for Nash to influence Red Dog and the other partners.

Although a large number of potential choices were discussed, five were central to the analysis:

1.  Nash could propose that technical teams from Nash and Red Dog work together and share intellectual property, with the goal of persuading Red Dog to proceed more aggressively. Although technical teams had been talking with one another, this would be a more formal study with a bigger scope.

2.  Nash could try to scale up by doing an equity swap with one of the other partners in the field. This would give Nash a larger stake in the field that would enable it to avoid blocking by the other partners in the field, and thus make an ambitious development program more feasible. Of course, Nash would have to give up equity in something of value that one of the other partners would want, and that could be difficult or unattractive.

3. Nash had several future development plans that could be proposed to the other JV partners. Nash could propose a bold development plan that had significant CAPEX associated with it. Or, Nash could propose a less ambitious development plan that would still seek to increase the extraction potential. And finally, Nash could simply agree to the current development plan for Charlie Brown.

4. Nash could, if agreement was lacking, threaten to veto future development plans, which would mean production would decline until there was agreement. This would have negative economic consequences for Nash, as well as Red Dog and the other partners. However, doing so could push Red Dog to be aligned with Nash.

5. Nash could do nothing, and just go along with whatever Red Dog wanted to do regarding production. Of course, this would mean picking status quo choices in the four decisions identified above. The outcome for doing this would need to be weighed against other possible outcomes in the game. This value could also be used as a proxy for the value Nash could receive from selling or swapping out its interest in Charlie Brown.

Whether Red Dog would agree or back down in response to Nash's offers or threats were choices that obviously needed to be considered in the game as well. Moreover, the choices in the game were not mutually exclusive. Different choices could be tried at different points in time. In addition, results from technical studies were due in about six months, and Nash could wait and choose some of its actions based on those results. For example, if Nash were to scale up early, before the studies showed additional reserves were more likely, the cost would be smaller than if Nash did so later. But of course, if Nash scaled up and the reserves were not there, it would be a regrettable decision.

The schematic game tree in Figure 7.1 shows the types of decisions Nash and the other players had and the learning event uncertainty, in a sequence thought to make the most

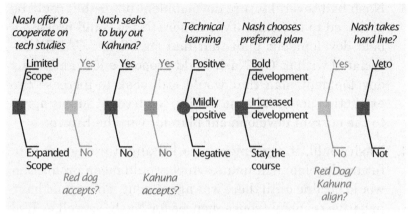

*Figure 7.1: Schematic Game Tree*

sense. (Of course, alternative sequences could be explored later in the analysis). We decided that the first choice had to do with whether to try to get cooperation on formal technical studies. Red Dog expressed interest in doing them, but wanted the studies to be somewhat limited. The Nash team thought the scope should be expanded to include an analysis of pipeline export alternatives. Since export capacity was currently limited, pipeline options could be important to expanding the extraction potential of the field. Whichever scope Nash offered, Red Dog could accept or reject.

The schematic game tree then shows a decision Nash has to scale up by acquiring the equity of one of the other partners in the Charlie Brown field, Kahuna, who can accept or reject Nash's offer. Obviously, this could be pursued later as well, but for now we thought it most reasonable to look at the decision as coming prior to the results of technical studies. After all, the Nash team believed strongly those results would be positive, and so Nash would want to avoid a blocking potential as well as the prospect of being forced to pay a very high price because the results were positive. Making the offer early could help Nash avoid being a hostage to the results.

After these decisions by Nash, Red Dog, and Kahuna, the schematic game tree shows the chance event of the technical learning. This could be positive, in which case there would be a strong case for an ambitious development plan but still no assurance of alignment with Red Dog and the other partners. The results could be negative, which would squelch even Nash's desire for a vigorous program. The median expectation was for results that would be in between, though more on the positive side. These would be results that would lead Nash toward pushing for a more ambitious plan than the current approach, but maybe not the boldest plan.

After the technical results are known, Nash would have certain options that would be influenced by the learning event. (Real options logic is thus built into the game.) It could choose:

♦ a bold development plan,

♦ a less ambitious but still increased development plan, or

♦ one that simply stays the course with the current development plan.

Red Dog could then align (or not) with Nash on whichever approach Nash pushes.

If Red Dog does not align with Nash, then Nash can choose to veto Red Dog's development plans.[1] Threatening to do so may cause Red Dog to align with Nash if the threat is seen to be credible. Although carrying through on the threat would involve an economic hit to Nash and the entire Charlie Brown JV, it could make sense and be perceived as credible. Red Dog as the operator, much more so than Nash, was keen to meet production targets that its people were accountable for. Hence, Red Dog was much more sensitive to meeting schedule than it was to revenue and profit.

When we completed the qualitative and quantitative analysis, we were able to develop a dynamic road map of the strategy and tactics Nash should pursue (see Figure 7.2). The first step was to request from Red Dog a joint study to not only assess the reservoir's potential on the geologic side, but also to study potential pipeline alternatives. What we realized too is that, up to this point, all discussions had been between

---

(1) If Kahuna's interest has not been bought out, Kahuna could also block Nash and/or Red Dog.

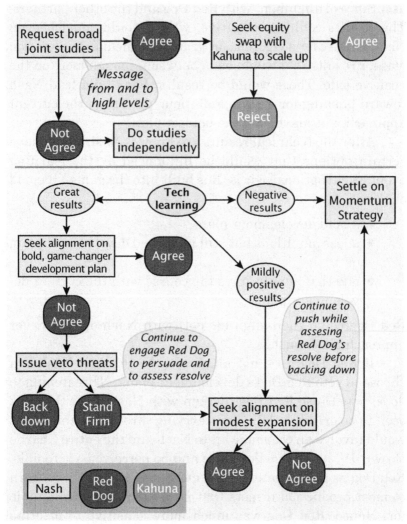

*Figure 7.2: Dynamic Road Map, Oil and Gas JV Case*
*(Although it is not shown in the figure, Kahuna's agreement would*
*also be necessary if Nash is unsuccessful in scaling up.)*

technical teams. This had two problems. For one, it limited the scope of what could be studied to the geologic side, and even there team members could not freely share intellectual property. Second, Red Dog had a highly top down organizational structure. Even if the technical teams could reach alignment, getting high level approval for a bottom up proposal would be difficult in Red Dog's organization. For these reasons, it was important to have the request come from very high level executives in Nash's organization to their counterparts in Red Dog. The work could thus be sanctioned by high-level executives from both companies to ensure that findings reached the top at both Nash and Red Dog. This would raise the level of seriousness of the study, and executives would be more committed to taking action than they otherwise would. It would also signal to Red Dog, early on, that Nash was keen to see that steps be taken to extract greater value from the Charlie Brown field. That signal could enhance credibility later on if a veto threat were needed.

If Red Dog did not agree to either the narrow or broader studies, Nash would undertake them independently. And regardless of whether an agreement could be reached with Red Dog, Nash would also pursue an equity swap with Kahuna to gain an additional 20% equity stake in Charlie Brown. If the offer was accepted, Nash could prevent the smaller partners from blocking Nash's more ambitious development plans. If the offer was not accepted, alignment with Kahuna would be necessary later.

The next part of the road map has to do with the technical learning. If the results showed a bounty of additional oil in the reservoir was highly probable, Nash would seek to have alignment on a bold, game-changer plan with Red Dog. If the results were mildly positive, Nash would seek a less ambitious but nonetheless augmented development plan. If negative results came out, Nash would simply support a stay-the-course approach.

Reaching alignment with Red Dog would be essential. Alignment with the smaller partners would only be necessary if Nash could not acquire Kahuna's 20% equity stake; if not, Kahuna was the key partner since only Kahuna had enough equity to block the plans.

If Nash pushed for a bold development plan and Red Dog rejected, Nash would then threaten to veto development plans. A veto would cause production to be halted until an agreement could be reached. Deferring production would cost money—time is money after all—but the value would not ultimately be lost. What was important to the threat was that the delay would not affect Nash as much as it would hurt Red Dog. In fact, if Nash had scaled up with Kahuna's equity, the delays would cost Nash even more money than they would cost Red Dog. However, because Red Dog was the operator, its people had a different metric than money. It was very important for Red Dog as the operator to produce to a schedule. If production slowed or stopped, then those in charge would be hurt dramatically within their organization for this presumed failure. Nash thus felt it had a very strong position, and the high value that could be attained with bolder approaches warranted a tough line. The long-term gains would far exceed the short-term losses.

If and when Nash were to stand firm, high-level management would engage their counterparts at Red Dog to persuade them as best as possible and to assess Red Dog's resolve. If the discussions suggested some softening, Nash would continue its hard line. If high-level executives from Red Dog appeared resolute for good reason (e.g., perhaps their hands were tied by the company's top officials), Nash could back down from its threat. Nash could ratchet its demands down by offering a more modest expansion of the development plan, and then slowly soften its position from there. In making concessions, though, Nash would be cognizant that doing so could have damaging reputational consequences later, and so the decisions needed to be made with great care.

In the end, Nash's client team got a great deal of value out of this. With Strategic Gaming, the analysis was grounded in numbers, much like one would do with decision analysis, and the client team was able to link strategy with tactics. Nash came to understand the issues needed to be elevated beyond that of the mid-level teams, which opened up much greater opportunities. And Nash was now armed with a clear plan of engagement, and had the economic modeling to make the case to Red Dog that there was a significant upside potential that both companies (and the other JV partners) could benefit from. Indeed, the projected value looking forward could more than double the $300 MM NPV expected for Charlie Brown compared with the momentum strategy. For Nash, successfully scaling up and gaining alignment on a bold development plan would mean the difference between making $100 MM and more than $250 MM. Even if Nash could not acquire Kahuna's equity and could only realize a modest increase to the development plan, there was still more than $30 MM of value for Nash to gain from a minimal CAPEX obligation.

On a number of other occasions Strategic Gaming has been employed to help oil and gas clients figure out how to deal with 3C issues in JVs, which are endemic to the industry. As with the case above, a collaborative deal is at the heart of these JVs. However, there regularly arise competitive and coordination issues as well. In another case, for instance, intra-JV differences over the value of drilling appraisal wells overlapped with concerns about a neighboring field that might develop faster and drain oil from the client's side of the reservoir. Other cases involved critical decisions about who to partner with or whether to end relationships that limit opportunity. In all of these cases, as in the one above, we had to understand the game's coordination and competitive issues, as well as the collaborative aspects, and often had to change the game to move more toward other corners of the 3C triangle.

*"Nevertheless, we must be prudent General.*
*We must never ignore the unknown, or the unpredictable."*
*– General Robert E. Lee to General Stonewall Jackson,*
*in the movie,* Gods and Generals

# 8
# Competitive Games

Competitive games are characterized by situations in which players have an incentive to win and a cooperative outcome is either unattractive or is not possible. Yet as we have seen in collaboration and coordination games, a situation that is predominantly a competitive game will often have elements of the other Cs, especially to the extent that changing the game toward a cooperative outcome makes sense. It is thus important to understand both the competitive risks the players face and to look broadly at both competitive and cooperative alternatives that are available to the players.

## High Tech Competitive Risk

Nash Tech was concerned about whether it could renew a lucrative supply contract for one of its key products, "x-factor," which it had held for five years. Nash feared that two potential competitors could develop a superior version of x-factor technology and wrestle the contract from Nash. Nash believed it would most likely have to innovate, and innovation would be very costly.

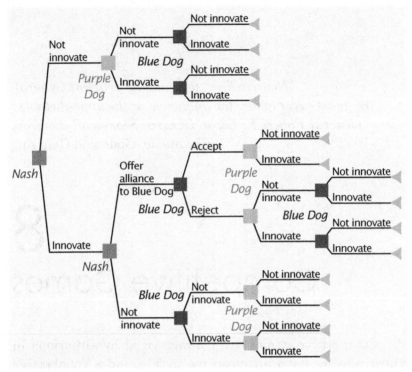

*Figure 8.1: Competition Example Game Tree*

As shown in the game tree in Figure 8.1, the key choice for Nash was to innovate or not, and for the two competitors, Blue Dog and Purple Dog, there was also an innovation choice. In addition, we realized in structuring the game that Nash could also offer an alliance to Blue Dog in lieu of costly innovation. In such an alliance, the two would partner on this type of technology and would not need to innovate significantly. Whatever costs there were would be shared. It was believed this alliance would make winning of the supply contract highly likely and the two might also gain from broader market capture with other potential customers. While there would be some value loss from splitting profits, it would likely be better than losing the contract.

The game tree shows all the choices as sequential, but in reality the innovation choices were simultaneous decisions. The players would make innovation decisions without knowledge of what the others were doing. (As discussed in chapter 3, we should draw information sets around the appropriate decision nodes to reflect this simultaneity, but to avoid confusion and show the structure of choices clearly, they are not shown in Figure 8.1.)

A key uncertainty not shown in the game tree, but that was an important assessment built into the economic model, was the probability that the customer would choose Nash or one of its competitors. This probabilistic assessment was conditional on whether Blue Dog, Purple Dog, and Nash innovated, and whether Nash and Blue Dog were in an alliance. The assessments showed that the customer was going to be quite biased in favor of Nash as the incumbent supplier:

♦ If Blue Dog and Purple Dog did not innovate, there was a probability of 1 that Nash would get the contract.

♦ If Blue Dog and/or Purple Dog innovated, and Nash did not, Nash's probability of winning the contract was about 0.4. Neither Blue Dog nor Purple Dog would have more than a probability 0.6 of winning.

♦ If all innovated, or if one of the competitors and Nash innovated, the probability of Nash receiving the contract would be 0.6. Each of the competitors thus had less than a 0.5 probability of winning the contract.

♦ If Nash was in an alliance with Blue Dog, and they did not innovate but Purple Dog did, they had a 0.6 probability of winning the contract.

As the customer was likely to be quite biased in favor of Nash, it turned out the costs to the other players of innovating in order to win the supply contract, which were expected to be substantially higher than Nash's would be, were not worth the risk. While they could spend money to innovate and try to win the supply contract, it would not be rational for them to do so, assuming that they shared Nash's assessments. In turn, Nash should not innovate.

The game matrix in Figure 8.2, though a bit more intricate than the 2 x 2 games discussed in Chapter 2, illustrates

| | Purple Dog: Not innovate<br>Blue Dog: Not innovate | Purple Dog: Not innovate<br>Blue Dog: Innovate | Purple Dog: Innovate<br>Blue Dog: Not innovate | Purple Dog: Innovate<br>Blue Dog: Innovate |
|---|---|---|---|---|
| Nash: Innovate | 0<br>0<br>234 | 0<br>-140<br>-174 | -205<br>0<br>189 | -235<br>-155<br>174 |
| Nash: Not innovate | 0<br>0<br>384 | 0<br>-125<br>309 | -190<br>0<br>324 | -205<br>-155<br>294 |

*Figure 8.2: Payoff Matrix*

this conclusion strongly. The matrix is now a 2 x 4 because there are 3 players, each with two strategic choices: innovate or not innovate. The way to read this is to think of it as two 2 x 2 games. In the four cells on the left hand side, Purple Dog has chosen to not innovate, and in the four cells on the right Purple Dog has chosen to innovate. Nash's expected value payoffs are in the bottom left of each cell, Blue Dog's are in the middle, and Purple Dog's are in the top right.

The only Nash equilibrium in the game is in the bottom left cell (shaded), where no player innovates. This is a best response for each player given that the others do not innovate. What is starkly clear from the matrix is that Blue Dog and Purple Dog never receive a payoff greater than 0. Whenever they innovate, they receive a negative payoff. That is because the numbers are expected values and the probabilities of their winning the supply contract are not large enough to make innovation worth the risk given the costs to innovate and the expected benefits. If Blue Dog and Purple Dog see the probabilities, costs, and benefits in a way that is roughly similar to how Nash modeled it, they would not innovate. Thus, the competitive risks Nash saw at the outset did not seem justified following the game analysis.

Of course, this conclusion depends on the other players seeing the game the way Nash did! This raises several issues that were important to deal with.

For one, Nash would have to think about tactics for engaging the potential competitors to convince them that the risks are substantial and to assess their thinking. We could not be sure how the competitors were thinking about the game. Perhaps they believed they would have a strong opportunity to capture the supply contract, and would be determined to proceed with costly innovation and compete with Nash. Hence, we discussed a range of messages that could be delivered, from posturing about how Nash was well-positioned to win the contract given incumbency advantages, to indicating that Nash was considering development of an x-factor plus. Such messages could come both in public forums (e.g., press releases) as well as direct engagement with the competitors. Both direct and indirect engagement could be useful and would be employed. However, direct discussions were seen as particularly valuable, for they would provide Nash an opportunity to simultaneously make its case and gauge the reactions of Blue Dog and Purple Dog to get a better sense about whether they were thinking about the game in the way Nash was.

Second, since there would always be some uncertainty about how the others players viewed the game, we also discussed offering a strategic alliance to Blue Dog. Though seemingly unnecessary given the game-theoretic result, this would provide Nash "insurance" given residual uncertainty about how the other players saw and would play the game. Nash could offer Blue Dog an alliance at a fairly low cost to deter Purple Dog from innovating when faced with what would now be very small odds of winning. Blue Dog could probably be persuaded to agree to the strategic alliance, meanwhile, because it would surely bring increased value with low risk, albeit less value than it would gain from winning the supply contract outright. For Nash, this would mean a value loss compared with going-it-alone, but the "insurance" could be worth it to avoid a very unprofitable outcome.

The execution plan made use of both the messaging tactics and the strategic alliance option, in sequence. By engaging in discussions with the competitors (Blue Dog in particular), Nash could assess their thinking. If Blue Dog or Purple Dog did not share Nash's view of the game and seemed determined to forge ahead and compete for the contract despite Nash's arguments, Nash could offer the strategic alliance to Blue Dog. In so doing, they would do modest innovation together, sharing the costs, and would make a strong public announcement of their partnership and intentions to deter Purple Dog from competing against what would be a virtually unbeatable alliance. Conversely, if Blue Dog seemed to be persuaded by Nash and reluctant to spend on innovation, Nash could avoid offering the strategic alliance.

The exercise thus led us to what was seen as a counterintuitive conclusion: Nash could probably avoid costly innovation and instead pursue more value-adding investments in its portfolio. Yet the exercise did more than that. In this case (as in many others), Strategic Gaming pointed to both a high-level strategic decision and to tactics that could elicit information and influence others. The dynamic road map provided learning opportunities to make a contingent strategic decision.

In other competitive cases, Strategic Gaming has helped companies see how cooperation through particular alliances could mitigate competitive risks or provide a competitive advantage. Other Strategic Gaming engagements revealed how the power of existing partners limited the ability to exercise, or the value of, competitive options. In turn, companies learned they had to work within constraints that had not been appreciated or were impelled to develop creative solutions to change the game. Some more strictly competitive scenarios, meanwhile, warranted the making of credible commitments to persuade competitors to "swerve," as in the game of Chicken. In short, Strategic Gaming has been applied to a wide range of competitive games, some with different types of cooperative dilemmas intermixed, and has helped companies understand the nature of these games and develop a proactive strategic and tactical plan of action to capture value.

Wherever in the 3C triangle a business situation has been, and where it has ended up, Strategic Gaming has helped companies realize billions of dollars of value. Yet to date, Strategic Gaming's use in the business world as a strategy tool is far from commonplace. The issue I now turn to is how you can make Strategic Gaming an integral and effective part of your business so that you and your company can be a step ahead of the competition and shape the game of business.

### Rethinking VOI: How the Game Changes Things

Decision analysis teaches us that the value of information (VOI) is either positive or zero. While the costs to obtain information may exceed the value to be gained, the value of the information itself is always nonnegative. The only debate is around how best to calculate the costs and benefits associated with the additional information. However, the notion that VOI is always positive can be dangerously misleading in the business world.

The interactive dimension that is often present in business situations can result in a negative VOI because other people or entities can take actions that negate the value of obtaining information. One reason has to do with timing. During the time it takes to gather information, another may capture a first-mover advantage that negates the potential benefit. A second reason is that others may learn from the information collected, which can lower the value of an opportunity by reducing informational advantages. These timing and informational issues are illustrated in the following example, which is based on simplified and disguised actual cases.

Nash Oil Company is considering whether to drill a second exploratory well in a block it owns. They do a traditional VOI analysis to figure out whether it is worthwhile. In the VOI analysis, the base value for the development without the second exploratory well has been calculated to be $300 MM. The well will cost $50 MM, and if it proves up positive re-

| | | Base NPV | Well Cost | Incremental NPV | Total |
|---|---|---|---|---|---|
| Drill second exploratory well | Success 0.25 | 300 | – 50 | + 500 | = 750 |
| | Failure 0.75 | 300 | – 50 | + 0 | = 250 |
| Develop now | | 300 | – 0 | + 0 | = 300 |

*Expected value of drilling is 0.25 x 750 + 0.75 x 250 = 375, which is 75 greater than the 300 from not drilling.*

*Figure A: Value of Information Decision Tree*

sults, Nash would be able to undertake an improved development plan that would result in $500 MM of additional value.

As shown in the decision tree in Figure A, Nash believes there is a 25% chance of success, which would yield $750 MM in value. Failure would net them $250 MM. Hence, the expected value of drilling is $375 MM, significantly greater than the $300 MM base value, so Nash should drill the exploratory well. That is the way traditional VOI analysis would go.

In this case, however, there is a broader game that changes the calculation for Nash. Kahuna Oil & Gas owns an adjacent block, and there has been talk between Nash and Kahuna about unitizing (combining) the two fields. On the other hand, Kahuna has recently been talking about moving to develop its block soon (independently of Nash).

By starting development soon, Kahuna would be able to drain some oil from the Nash side of the reservoir unless Nash also develops its field quickly. Drainage would transfer about $150 MM in value from Nash to Kahuna, creating motivation for Kahuna to develop quickly. Nash could be similarly motivated, as Nash could drain $50 MM in value from Kahuna's side of the reservoir if it develops quickly and Kahuna does not.

The decisions facing Nash and Kahuna, and the associated payoffs to these players, are illustrated with the game tree shown in Figure B. Remember that game trees are similar to decision trees, but model the actions of other players as decisions (rather than uncertainties), and each player's decisions are a function of others' decisions and their own payoffs (value).

| | | Develop... | NPV | Drainage Nash Effect | Nash Total | Base Drainage NPV | Kahuna Effect | Kahuna Total |
|---|---|---|---|---|---|---|---|---|
| | Kahuna | Now | 750 | -150 | = 600 | 200 | +150 | = 350 |
| Drill second exploratory well | Success 0.25 | Later | 750 | -0 | = 750 | 200 | +0 | = 200 |
| | Kahuna | Now | 250 | -150 | = 100 | 200 | +150 | = 350 |
| | Failure 0.75 | Later | 250 | -0 | = 250 | 200 | +0 | = 200 |
| Develop now | Develop now | | 300 | +0 | = 300 | 200 | -0 | = 200 |
| Kahuna | Develop later | | 300 | +50 | = 350 | 200 | -50 | = 150 |

*Nash*

*Expected value of drilling is 0.25 x 600 + 0.75 x 100 = 225, which is less than the 300 from not drilling.*

## Figure B: Value of Information Game Tree

In the game tree, we see that Kahuna will always have an incentive to "Develop now," either to reap the rewards of draining the Nash side of the reservoir or to avoid being drained. Because Kahuna should develop now, choosing to delay development by drilling the second exploratory well is likely to cost Nash $150 MM in value, whether the well is a success or not. Thus, the expected value of drilling the exploratory well has dropped from $375 MM in the decision analysis to $225 MM in the game analysis, less than the $300 MM from developing now.

Contrary to the conclusion of the decision analysis, then, Nash should develop now and avoid drainage, which will net $300 MM NPV. The first-mover advantage we see in the game means that the information has negative value and reverses the recommendation we would make in a traditional VOI analysis.

A second reason information may have negative value is that the information may become known to other players, who can then use that information to their advantage. In this example, Kahuna would likely discover something about the results of a second exploratory well. If the well is a success, Nash would announce the results. If it fails, Nash would say little, if anything. This silence would be a clear signal to Kahuna.

In this case, the seeking of information could affect whether Nash and Kahuna can agree on a unitization of their respective blocks into a single development. While all players recognize unitization could be a great cost-saving measure, doing so requires agreement on the equity split and a host of other terms. With a positive test result, Nash is likely to want a large share of the equity. That sort of equity split, while based on data about reserves, might not be acceptable to Kahuna's management. Hence, the risk of a highly unequal equity split may give Kahuna more incentive to develop its own block separately and quickly.

Taking all these considerations into account, Kahuna has strong reasons to develop quickly and should stand firm against any strong demands Nash might make in unitization discussions. While a second exploratory well could show that it is more "fair" for Nash to have a predominant part of the equity split in a unitization, fairness is beside the point. The ability to move quickly gives Kahuna significant bargaining leverage. Nash should not, therefore, let the significant value uplift potential they see from a second exploratory well cloud its judgment about commercial realities.

In this example, then, we have seen how two key game dimensions—timing and information—can make VOI negative. The notion that information cannot have negative value can, in fact, be dangerously misleading. Indeed, in the example above, being concerned about VOI without first securing unitization would be a strategic blunder. Instead of accepting the received wisdom, analysts need to pay heed to interactive issues, for the game can drastically change analytical needs and strategy prescriptions.

# Part IV: Conclusion

*"You can't do big things as a competitor if you're content with doing things only a little better than the competition."*
– William C. Taylor and Polly LaBarre, in Mavericks at Work: Why the Most Original Minds in Business Win

*"Drive thy business or it will drive thee."*
– Benjamin Franklin

# 9

# Integrating Strategic Gaming into Your Business

Savvy executives know that they need to structure and analyze situations but not subject themselves and their teams to paralysis by analysis. They cannot afford to get bogged down in endless discussions about whether an analytical model uses all the right assumptions and perfectly captures every detail. No model does. Executives need quick, reliable, and value-adding insights that foster team alignment, provide the confidence to move forward in risky environments, and are actionable.

Strategic Gaming is designed to meet these needs. It helps companies efficiently gain keen insight into any issue in which the actions of competitors, partners, and other players can have an important impact. Indeed, Strategic Gaming has added billions of dollars of value on a wide range of business strategy issues.

Though game theory is applicable to a myriad of interactive business issues that pose difficult competitive-cooperative dilemmas, and many companies often find themselves faced with such situations, game theory applications have been relatively minimal and the integration of game theory into decision-making processes is virtually non-existent. This situation is unfortunate, for companies are leaving significant value on the table.

This chapter discusses how Strategic Gaming can be integrated into your business so that you can systematically apply it to effectively and practically tackle dilemmas of competition and cooperation. In some cases, this will involve simply recognizing the need and applying the approach on an ad hoc basis. In other cases, a formal strategic decision-making process should be refined. In all cases, the answer begins with diagnosis.

## Diagnosing Game Issues

At the simplest level, *influence* is the key to understanding whether Strategic Gaming is applicable to an issue. Do we have the ability to influence others to enhance the value we realize? Can others influence us and impact the value we get? If the answer to either or both of these questions is yes, Strategic Gaming may add valuable insights.

A more sophisticated understanding of Strategic Gaming's applicability involves consideration of whether game issues can have a significant impact on a project, business, product, or asset. In a diagnostic tool colleagues and I have developed for use with clients, we call this impact Interaction Risk (IR). Quite simply, IR is a quantification of how much value is at risk due to the mismanagement of interactions with other players.

Estimating IR is straightforward. First ask, what is the potential value (e.g., NPV) of a project, business, product, or asset? If your industry is capital intensive and you do not have a reasonable estimate of value, determine how much CAPEX you would expect to be involved.

Second, think about the various consequences of player interactions. Can mismanagement of player interactions lead to any or all of the following:

♦ Delays,
♦ Worsened competitive position (getting blindsided or outmaneuvered, winding up in a weak position),
♦ Poor deals (inadequate terms, leaving value on the table),
♦ Reputational damage,
♦ Partner (supplier) mismanagement, or
♦ Missed opportunities?

Third, by thinking about these potential consequences, ask what percentage of your project, business, product, or asset value might be at risk if competitive positioning or interactions with other players are mismanaged. For example, if your project has a potential value of $150 MM and you believe that 20% of the value could be at risk from such consequences, your IR is $30 MM.

The IR is most useful for estimating whether an application of Strategic Gaming is worth the effort. If the IR is small relative to the size of the overall value, you may prefer not to use Strategic Gaming. But if the IR is, say, $100 MM of a $500 MM opportunity, a rigorous game analysis to capture as much value as possible is clearly warranted.

Calculating IR is useful not only for evaluating individual opportunities. Considering the frequency with which project-level IRs are material can also provide insight into whether one needs to integrate the approach more fully into decision-making processes.

Beyond calculating IR, the diagnostic tool mentioned above can help one reach a better understanding of whether, when, and to what extent Strategic Gaming should be employed. For a description and download instructions, see the Appendix.

## Decision-making Processes and Strategic Gaming

Integrating Strategic Gaming into a company's strategic decision-making process will make project, business, product, or asset strategies more commercially focused from an early stage through to implementation, enabling the capture of value and reducing IR. Delays and value drain from partner misalignment will be limited, competitive blind spots and the risk of being outmaneuvered will be minimized, and the ability to recognize and take advantage of commercial opportunities will be enhanced.

How can this be accomplished? First, consider what strategy process or processes exist and thus how Strategic Gaming can be made part of a formalized process. In some cases, formal processes are minimal or non-existent, so ad hoc use of Strategic Gaming and other tools and approaches may be the best solution. In other cases, a highly structured decision-making process will need refinement to ensure that Strategic Gaming is employed as appropriate.

Smaller companies typically have no formal decision-making process for framing and evaluating strategic decisions. Given the nature and relatively small number of big and important strategy decisions they need to make, analytical tools can easily be employed as appropriate on an ad hoc basis. Of course, executives of smaller companies should do the best they can in making decisions, and so being aware of Strategic Gaming and diagnosing whether there is significant IR will help them to understand if game-theoretic analysis is warranted in making an important decision.

Most large companies have some formal decision-making processes, although these are typically not appropriate for making decisions where there is significant IR. For instance, many use Six Sigma and Stage-Gate processes, which are more focused on having efficient and effective manufacturing and business operational processes than on making strategy and commercial decisions. Other companies have quantitative strategic decision-making processes based on decision analysis or traditional valuation methods that ignore and are ill-suited for unraveling interactive dynamics. Incorporating Strategic Gaming as part of any of these decision-making processes should be highly complementary to what is done already, for all are concerned with using quantitative measures and a disciplined approach to making better decisions and improving outcomes.

At a conceptual level, Strategic Gaming can be made part of an existing process without great difficulty. Although incorporation of Strategic Gaming as part of an existing process will require some tailoring to determine where and how it should fit within current processes, this should be fairly straightforward.

Seven guidelines should be employed to develop and refine a strategic decision-making process that includes Strategic Gaming:

1. *Encourage broad scoping of issues.* All too often, decision-making processes encourage users to narrowly define an issue prematurely, and as such they often leave out important potential factors. This is particularly true with respect to interactive dynamics.

   For instance, Nash may be concerned about ways to make Asset X more profitable, but at the same time Black Dog may be concerned about how Asset X affects Assets Y and Z, and vice versa. Black Dog could thus take actions or react to Nash's moves, which would impact Nash's value for Asset X. Likewise, Nash's moves may impact Assets Y and Z. If the scope is too narrow, Nash will have a dangerous competitive blind spot. To avoid such situations, a strategic decision-making process needs to ensure that project teams think broadly about the scope of their work from the start.

   To help with scoping problems broadly, one useful method is to do a "fried-egg" diagram, as shown in Figure 9.1. In this, Nash's concern, Asset X, is in the center, but the next circle shows Assets Y and Z to be part of a broader scope. Rather than focus on one asset, the analysis would consider the three assets together.

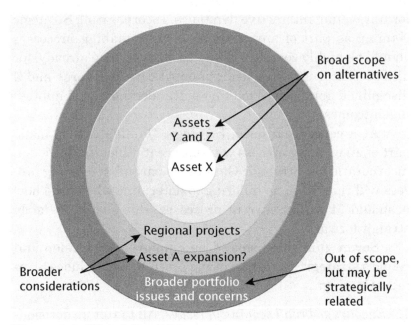

*Figure 9.1: "Fried Egg" Diagram*

Moving further out, we would also consider the impact of other regional projects and the potential expansion of Asset A on Nash's and Black Dog's potential strategies. Such broader considerations would make it into quantitative analysis in only a high-level way, if at all.

Finally, we would typically want to discuss broader portfolio concerns that Nash and Black Dog would have. This would not be part of quantitative work, but should be an integral part of strategy development. We would look at what the game analysis tells us about Nash's and Black Dog's strategic alternatives, and ask ourselves whether in fact the players would choose a particular path given their broader considerations. For example, we might find in the game analysis that it is better for Black Dog to pursue Alternative A over Alternative B because our economic model finds a $10 MM benefit. However, in the bigger picture, Alternative A may have a serious negative impact on Black Dog that is obvious but is not part of the economic model. Hence, by bringing in the broader portfolio concerns of both players, we can avoid blind spots that could lead us astray.

2. *Diagnosis is essential.* As discussed above, understanding whether Strategic Gaming would be useful is important. This will likely be missed if the scope is not defined broadly enough (as point 1 discusses). But diagnosis can go beyond identifying IR and the need for Strategic Gaming. It should help us understand what methodologies need to be employed and the nature of analysis that needs to be undertaken. So, for example, the diagnosis may address whether options need to be modeled or a straightforward decision analysis is sufficient. It may also help us understand whether we need to engage in significant quantitative work or whether it would not be worth the effort. Often analysts spend many hours building large, complex economic models to address issues of relatively little value. Such a poor use of limited resources can be avoided with simple diagnosis that has an eye toward value.

3. *Don't apply a hammer to everything.* As the discussion on diagnosis suggests, there are different methodologies for different business problems. And just as you wouldn't want to hire a handyman who has only a hammer in his toolbox, you should not apply decision analysis, Strategic Gaming, real options, or any other tool to every business problem.

4. *Use a clear, consistent approach.* While a company should have expertise in multiple methodologies, and innovation in applying these methodologies should be encouraged, it is dangerous to have competing methodologies. There are, for instance, alternative methodologies that call themselves "real options." These have different requirements and approaches, and can produce different outputs and recommendations. Similarly, others who use game theory in the business world have much different approaches than Strategic Gaming—these tend to be black-box approaches, are not very quantitative, or are highly academic. When

considering real options, game theory, and other methods, it is very important to choose based on what is best for the types of issues a company faces and what would complement existing processes and capabilities. It is obviously far better to build on a company's strengths and existing capabilities than to employ a much different methodology. For example, if a company has a strong capability in decision analysis, a black-box game-theoretic approach without a quantitative methodology will have limited credibility and be seen to be of limited utility. Allowing or encouraging methodology competition within an organization promotes confusion and inconsistency, and inhibits the mastering of a methodology and its integration. A company that can settle on particular methodologies and stick with them over the long haul will have the greatest chance of seeing their applications be effective and flourish within the organization.

5. *Academic roots are great, but be practical.* When academic purity is over-emphasized, game theory and other decision-making applications can easily become overly complex and impractical. Strong academic expertise and methodologies are important, but they must be coupled with a practical approach and deep, hands-on experience.

6. *Transparency is essential.* Black-box business applications are unnecessary and of limited usefulness. In fact, lack of transparency should be seen as a sign that the underpinning methodology is suspect. Executives should demand that recommendations and the analytics that support them be transparent so that they can have confidence in, and ownership of, the results. This will enable executives to more effectively implement strategies and tactics and to quickly adjust to changing circumstances.

7. *Encourage quantitative analysis, with limits.* The proper use of quantitative methods such as decision analysis, real options, and Strategic Gaming is tremendously powerful in adding clarity and value. Not thinking through the num-

bers in a disciplined way is simply guesswork and is all too common. In some cases, the judicious use of qualitative shortcuts can be useful, but more often shortcuts sacrifice important and reliable insights that erode value.

On the other hand, I have seen numerous quantitative studies that were overkill. Analysts sometimes spend months, even years, building elegant and detailed economic models that consume tens of megabytes of hard drive space and are so big they have to run on servers rather than a PC. For strategy issues, that is nonsensical. These models do no better than simple models do in addressing strategy questions, and in fact they make it difficult if not impossible to tease insights out of them. All a strategy model can or should do is provide a good sense of magnitude and direction, and help promote a sensible conversation about strategy. Strategy models cannot and will not give a precise prediction of how much a particular strategy is worth, and striving for precision is counterproductive. So while quantitative analysis can add great value, it should not be done at an overly detailed level.

Beyond using these guidelines to refine and incorporate Strategic Gaming into a decision-making process, two broad tasks need to be undertaken to integrate Strategic Gaming effectively: education and the creation of an infrastructure of experts.

The purpose of education is twofold: to build awareness and to enhance capabilities. There is a need to build the Strategic Gaming market within an organization, for most people know little or nothing about game theory, how and where it can be applied practically, and what the incremental benefits are. Regular presentations about Strategic Gaming in different parts of an organization to discuss the approach and report on results of its application will go a long way toward building awareness and credibility. To the extent a variety of people, speaking from different perspectives, can be involved in these presentations, credibility of the message will be enhanced and the capability for applying and integrating Strategic Gaming will grow.

Formal training is another part of the educational effort. I have given three-hour workshops to as many as 200 people, and three-day seminars to 10 or 20 employees of a company. The short workshops for large audiences tend to work like presentations, increasing awareness and teaching people a few important lessons.

The more rigorous training found in three-day seminars enables a deeper understanding of what Strategic Gaming is about. Participants can methodically work through and discuss the content in this book and engage in a case exercise to gain something akin to hands-on experience and understanding. Such seminars build awareness at a deeper level and enable participants to go back to their day jobs and apply Strategic Gaming to a number of relatively simple but common issues. It will also change the way they think about their jobs and issues that come before them. Although they will be unable to tackle the most complex issues with Strategic Gaming after just three days, they will be aware of the need and seek out appropriate expertise. And if they work on the issues side-by-side with Strategic Gaming experts, they will be more valuable partners in the exercise and enhance their learning.

In addition to education within an organization, developing an infrastructure of experts within a company is very important. Such an approach has been a staple of Six Sigma, and has had much to do with its success. In Six Sigma, there are "Champions," "Master Black Belts," "Black Belts," "Green Belts," and "Yellow Belts." Each has different roles and levels of expertise, and as this infrastructure grows, Six Sigma becomes an integral part of a company.

For Strategic Gaming, I see three levels as appropriate for creating such an infrastructure:

1. *Gaming Ambassadors.* These are people who have some experience with Strategic Gaming on projects and have some formal training. They are able to diagnose business issues and understand if and how game theory may be a relevant tool (and one worth applying).

2. *Game Framers.* Game Framers are specialists who have an ability not only to diagnose but to scope issues broadly to incorporate game dynamics and to structure game interactions to draw out qualitative insights. Their work can help develop the scope of how initial economic models get built and set up later game analysis.

3   *Strategic Gaming Practitioners.* Those who have engaged in formal training and done apprenticeships on Strategic Gaming exercises reach a level of mastery that qualifies them to take the lead in applying the methodology to projects.

## The Leadership Difference

Strategic Gaming provides a way to think through action-reaction dynamics in a rigorous yet practical way that is more effective than what can be done with other methodologies. Indeed, Strategic Gaming can provide companies with a uniquely valuable competitive advantage, particularly if it is integrated into a company's strategic decision-making process. The discussion above shows how it is possible to do so by following seven basic guidelines, engaging in various forms of education, and creating an infrastructure of experts. But to make it all happen and seize a unique and valuable competitive advantage requires leadership.

Executive leadership needs to come from various levels of an organization. Analytical experts within an organization need to pursue innovation with Strategic Gaming. Their vision and support will provide essential credibility and input into integration efforts. Various executives throughout an organization who have used Strategic Gaming can also support innovation. Their role as consumer advocates will help build organizational credibility.

Ultimately the executive leadership of a company needs to have the vision, commit the resources, and empower managers and technical experts to integrate Strategic Gaming into decision-making processes. Although it will not happen overnight, a strong, sustained commitment will transform an organization's mind-set, capabilities, and ways of doing business. By doing so, a top-notch executive team can ensure that its company stays a step ahead of the competition, captures value, and minimizes interaction risks.

# Appendix
## Game Theory Diagnostic Tool

My firm has developed a diagnostic tool for helping our clients understand whether, when, and to what extent game theory/Strategic Gaming should be employed. The tool, in Excel 2003 and Excel 2007, can be downloaded at my firm's web site, www.stratgaming.com/help.html.

The diagnostic makes two primary types of assessments. First, it evaluates the level of "influence complexity" and "interaction risk" value to make a preliminary assessment about how extensive a gaming effort should be involved, if any. That is, does the project need a modest or a serious amount of framing and structuring (if influence complexity is relatively low or high)? Does any game framing need to be tied to minimal ("back-of-the-envelope") valuation modeling or significant quantitative valuation efforts (based on a high "interaction risk")?

Second, for issues where gaming appears to be a useful tool, the diagnostic gives a preliminary estimate of when analysis should begin. Users of the tool can then see where, in their project planning, they might bring gaming into the analysis to be of greatest value.

The diagnostic also addresses two related, and important, framing questions. First, it provides a recommendation about whether you need to consider and evaluate future options. Option value is related to the gaming context because options are often contingent on interactions with other players (e.g., one cannot exercise a future option if another player takes some action that removes the option). Full and accurate evaluation of some projects requires incorporating an estimate of the project's impact on other assets and opportunities. The diagnostic provides a recommendation about whether your project needs to take a broad frame, incorporating other parts of the value chain in your framing, alternative generation, and evaluation. These considerations are incorporated in the diagnostic because they have been important issues in a number of projects we have worked.

The diagnostic has six sets of questions, which are used with the following logic:

1. Project value:

   a. Estimated value (or CAPEX) of the project, from <$50 MM to >$4 billion: in general, this is used to help understand the extent of any effort. Small projects with little at risk should require less effort than high value projects with a lot at risk.

   b. The amount of value that would need to be gained or lost to appear on management's radar screen. This is to help assess whether Interaction Risk is a significant concern.

2. Identify decisions with an interactive component:

   a. Types of decisions by you and one or more other players. This is used to determine the extent of influence complexity/gaming effort.

   b. Timing for when the issue/decision should be resolved. This is to help understand the timing of analysis.

      (i) For each of the interactive decisions identified, there is a recommendation for when to start game framing. This is based firstly on what time frame the issue needs to be resolved:

      (1) If less than 1 year, begin immediately

      (2) If between 1 and 3 years, begin gaming analysis within 1 year

      (3) If greater than 3 years, talk to SGG about timing.

      (ii) One important caveat to these rules, however, is that if the user identifies interdependencies of their project with other assets/opportunities, the diagnostic will suggest that gaming analysis start immediately.

The rationale for this is that the frame needs to be relatively broad and include interactive dynamics. To start the gaming later could lead to a too narrow and misleading scope and results, and a significant amount of re-work later on.

3. Strategic Value: Whether the project is interdependent with other assets/opportunities, for you and/or other players. The purpose of this is to understand whether a broad or a narrow frame should be used, and whether it would make sense to begin gaming soon (as part of a broad frame). If one's frame is too narrow from the start, analysis will miss key factors and results will be biased.

    a. NOTE: The diagnostic will deem influence complexity to be in the high range if:

        *(i)* 2 or more interactive decisions are identified, or if

        *(ii)* The project is interdependent with other assets (for you and/or other players).

4. Future Options: These questions consider the possibility of learning/flexibility and whether evaluation of options needs to be done in a gaming context. The responses here are reflected in the recommendation, but do not show up in the table or with respect to timing.

5. Identify the types of risks involved if player interactions are not managed effectively. This is used to help the user understand the potential portion of value that is at risk due to player interactions. It may also prove useful for communicating the implications of the diagnostic to other team members or to management. By itself, it does not produce any output.

6. Identify the portion of the total value (or CAPEX) that may be at risk due to stakeholder interactions. This percentage is multiplied by the value estimated in question 1. If the resulting "interaction risk" is greater than the amount that would appear on management's radar screen, the interaction risk will be deemed high (thus putting the project in one of the two right quadrants of the output table).

Users can and should insert the diagnostic's timing recommendations into a project plan and/or consult with others as appropriate.

Any questions about the diagnostic should be brought to the attention of SGG, info@stratgaming.com.

# References

Amram, Martha and Nalin Kulatilaka. 1999. *Real Options: Managing Strategic Investment in an Uncertain World* (Boston: Harvard Business School Press).

Axelrod, Robert. 1984. *The Evolution of Cooperation* (New York: Basic Books).

Brandenburger, Adam M. and Barry J. Nalebuff. 1996. *Co-Opetition* (New York: Doubleday).

Clemen, Robert T. 1997. *Making Hard Decisions*, Second Edition (Cincinnati: Southwestern College Publishing).

Dixit, Avinash K. and Barry J. Nalebuff. 1991. *Thinking Strategically: The Competitive Edge in Business, Politics, and Everyday Life* (New York and London: W.W. Norton & Company).

Fisher, Roger, William Ury and Bruce Patton. 1991. *Getting to Yes: Negotiating Agreement Without Giving In*, Second Edition (New York: Penguin Books).

Fudenberg, Drew, and Jean Tirole. 1991. *Game Theory* (Cambridge: The MIT Press).

Howard, R.A. and J.E. Matheson. 1984. "Influence Diagrams." In R.A. Howard and J.E. Matheson (eds.), *Readings on the Principles and Applications of Decision Analysis*, Volume 2 (Menlo Park, CA: Strategic Decisions Group): 719-762.

Kreps, David M. 1990. *A Course in Microeconomic Theory* (Princeton: Princeton University Press).

Leach, Patrick. 2006. *Why Can't You Just Give Me the Number?* (Sugar Land, TX: Probabilistic Publishing).

McMillan, John. 1992. *Games, Strategies & Managers* (New York: Oxford University Press).

McNamee, Peter and John Celona. 2001. *Decision Analysis for the Professional*, Third Edition (Menlo Park, CA: SmartOrg, Inc.).

Morrow, James D. 1994. *Game Theory for Political Scientists* (Princeton: Princeton University Press).

Nasar, Sylvia. 1998. *A Beautiful Mind* (New York: Simon & Schuster).

Osborne, Martin J. and Ariel Rubinstein. 1994. *A Course in Game Theory* (Cambridge, MA: The MIT Press).

Pahre, Robert and Paul A. Papayoanou. 1997. "Using Game Theory to Link Domestic and International Politics." *Journal of Conflict Resolution*, 41, 1 (February): 4-11.

Porter, Michael E. 1980. *Competitive Strategy* (New York: The Free Press).

Rasmusen, Eric. 1989. *Games and Information: An Introduction to Game Theory* (Oxford: Basil Blackwell).

The Royal Swedish Academy of Sciences. 2005. "Press Release: The Bank of Sweden Prize in Economic Sciences in Memory of Alfred Nobel 2005." (October 10). http://nobelprize.org/nobel_prizes/economics/laureates/2005/press.html

Schelling, Thomas C. 1960. *The Strategy of Conflict* (Cambridge and London: Harvard University Press).

Skinner, David C. 2009. *Introduction to Decision Analysis*, Third Edition (Sugar Land, TX: Probabilistic Publishing).

Stein, Arthur A. 1992. "Coordination and Collaboration: Regimes in an Anarchic World." *International Organization* 36 (Spring): 299-324.

Stein, Arthur A. 1990. *Why Nations Cooperate: Circumstance and Choice in International Relations* (Ithaca: Cornell University Press).

Tsebelis, George. 1989. "The Abuse of Probability in Political Analysis: The Robinson Crusoe Fallacy." *American Political Science Review* 83, 1 (March): 77-91.

Tversky, Amos and Daniel Kahneman. 1986. "Rational Choice and the Framing of Decisions." In Robin M. Hogarth and Melvin W. Reder (eds.), *Rational Choice: The Contrast between Economics and Psychology* (Chicago: University of Chicago Press): 67-84.

# Index

# Biography
## Paul Papayoanou

Dr. Paul Papayoanou is the founder of SGG. He developed and trademarked the practical application of game theory known as Strategic Gaming®, which he and his firm use to help large and small companies in oil and gas, electric power, alternative energy, manufacturing, financial services, high tech, and the life sciences to develop business and negotiation strategies. He also employs decision analysis, real options, and war gaming tools, teaches Strategic Gaming and game theory techniques to executives, and leads the firm's unique capabilities in political risk assessment.

Dr. Papayoanou has been using game theory approaches in academia and the business world for more than 20 years. He received a Ph.D. from UCLA in 1992, and was a professor at the University of California, San Diego and at Harvard University. He then developed the Strategic Gaming approach and Game Solver computer program, which he has used in his own consulting practices and as leader of Strategic Decisions Group's Strategic Gaming practice.

Dr. Papayoanou has lectured about Strategic Gaming at the Harvard Business School. He has also given speeches and provided training to hundreds of energy, financial, manufacturing, and life science executives, as well as Latin American political and business leaders, on applying Strategic Gaming to business strategy, negotiations, M&A work, auction bidding strategies, political strategy, and on how to create win-wins in the workplace.

Dr. Papayoanou is the author of a book, *Power Ties*, and co-editor and contributor to *New Games*, a special issue of *The Journal of Conflict Resolution*. He has also written numerous articles that have appeared in journals, books, and business publications.

Made in the USA
Monee, IL
08 April 2021